KNOT THE ONE

Why Getting Dumped Before My Wedding was the Best Thing that Ever Happened to Me

STACEY BECKER

Thought Catalog Books
Brooklyn, NY

THOUGHT CATALOG BOOKS

Copyright © 2015 by Stacey Becker

All rights reserved. Published by Thought Catalog Books, a division of The Thought & Expression Co., Williamsburg, Brooklyn. For general information and submissions: manuscripts@thoughtcatalog.com.

First edition, 2015
ISBN 978-0692562529
10 9 8 7 6 5 4 3 2 1

Founded in 2010, Thought Catalog is a website and imprint dedicated to your ideas and stories. We publish fiction and non-fiction from emerging and established writers across all genres.

Cover image by © iStockPhoto.com/cclickclick
Cover design by Daniella Urdinlaiz

CHAPTER 1

When people asked us later how we met, we almost always said that it was at the airport. At one point we had all the details nailed down—from the time we noticed each other in the security line, to the point where he found out his flight was delayed and came over to my gate to "kill some time." In some versions he invites me to join him for a drink in the food court. In other versions he makes up a question about the laptop he sees me using. In all the versions, he gets my phone number and impulsively calls me five minutes later to ask me out. He probably saw this happen on a cell phone commercial at some point and thought it seemed romantic. If analyzed critically and taken apart, this story of how we met doesn't really make sense. But nobody seems to care that the shuttle flight terminal at Washington, DC's National Airport to Boston and New York is not located next to the outbound flights to California. I hated lying to people about it, but it was easier than explaining to our parents that online dating was the norm these days.

I had practically sworn off online dating by the time I came across Brad's profile. It seemed pointless. You see a picture of an attractive person, you try to make witty conversation over email and hope this will lead to a text, phone call, or actual plans. While getting to the plans phase, you try to sound down-to-earth yet intriguing, friendly but not desperate and hope for just a second that this stranger is The One. You struggle over a mutually convenient place to meet up—a public place to avoid being mugged or killed by a total lunatic posing as a promising prospect. You want the place to offer the option of drinks and dinner—drinks so that if you are not interested, you're at least buzzed and can run off safely to the nearest Metro station, calling your friend on the way to go over every horrid detail of the date; dinner so that if things are going well, you have the option of staying longer. You change clothing multiple times before venturing out, not wanting to appear too trendy, too lawyerly (several guys have told me straight up that they don't like lawyers, nor would they ever want to date one), too slutty, too conservative. Once you pick the outfit, the meeting spot, and the time—you get there and notice several extremely good-looking single guys giving you a smile and for a second, you pray, beg, plead that one of these guys could be YOUR guy, but he never is. Then your date shows up and he is five inches shorter than stipulated in his profile, looks nothing like his photo and seems almost as annoyed to be there as you are that he's not what you were hoping for.

The night I was supposed to meet Brad for the first time, I had just flown back to DC from a business trip in New York. I had seen his profile about two weeks earlier and learned enough about him (including multiple photos from multiple angles) to want to know more. We exchanged several emails and decided to meet on a Thursday night, but this last-minute business trip had made our plans tentative. On the cab ride from the airport to my apartment in Dupont Circle, I sent Brad an email saying that I was exhausted—that perhaps we could reschedule. Thirty seconds later, he was calling my cell phone.

"What? Canceling on me before you get to know me? You have to meet me first before you decide to stand me up," the voice said.

"Brad?" I smiled. "You got my email. Don't take it personally, OK? I've been up since 5:00 AM and am afraid I wouldn't be very good company tonight."

"Well, how about this?" he responded. "Let's move our meeting spot to Buffalo Billiards—it's much closer than that bar in Georgetown, and we can just meet for one drink. If you don't like me after that, we'll call it a night. No offense taken."

"Wow, that sounds like a good deal. Can you give me thirty minutes to change and get myself over there?"

"Of course," he said. "In fact, that will give me time to finish giving myself a haircut. See you in thirty."

Before I could react to that last comment, he was off the phone and my cab was in front of my building. I wondered what kind of person cuts his own hair. Maybe he was balding or really cheap. Maybe he just needed a trim in the front—did he have bangs? I figured that I only had to stick around for one drink to uncover these mysteries.

I dressed quickly in a pair of dark jeans and a casual long sleeved, fitted green top, nice enough that it looked like I was trying, simple enough to show I wasn't trying too hard. I walked the seven minutes over to Buffalo Billiards and descended the stairs to the large open space of pool tables and lounge chairs. I saw Brad right away—he had a big grin on his face when our eyes met, and his hair had a very short buzz cut look. His ears stuck out a little too much, but his big blue friendly eyes and smile made up for them.

As my immediate reaction was not, "Should I call my sister and have her fake an emergency to get out of here?" I knew it was a good sign. After our initial greeting to one another, we ordered drinks and agreed to play a game of pool.

When our beers arrived, Brad said, "Why don't you tell me the story of your life?"

I looked at him, wondering whether he was kidding—but he looked pretty sincere.

"Wow," I responded. "That's a pretty tall order."

He smiled and said, "Well, then, you better make it interesting."

I decided to keep it short and sweet, stopping in between segments of my life to see if he was paying attention. He asked me several questions along the way, which I answered succinctly and truthfully and suddenly, I realized something—I was actually enjoying myself.

Brad was 25, loved his college football team, playing golf and taking care of his car. He also loved to cook, was obsessed with keeping his room clean and had a deep appreciation of country music. After a couple more beers, we were definitely flirting, and as we left the bar, he took my hand to walk me back to my apartment building. We didn't say much initially. We just kept walking, hand in hand, enjoying the anticipation of the end of a great first date.

We arrived in front of my building, and I told him it was time for me to go in.

"Let's go out to Adams Morgan," he said. "There's this Irish pub there having trivia night. It could be fun."

"I'm sure it would be," I said, "But I like how tonight has gone so far, and I'd like to end it on a high note."

"What does that mean?" he said, with the big smile coming back. "Are you scared of trivia?"

"Terrified, actually," I responded. "Truthfully, it's just that I've had my fair share of great first dates, and I'd like this one to actually lead to a second date. I think my chances for that greatly increase if I say goodnight right now."

"Why do I have to be the first guy you're testing this theory on?" he said with a smile.

"You're just lucky, I guess," I said.

We chatted a little bit more about our upcoming plans for the next few days. Thanksgiving was right around the corner and we were both going home for it.

He asked me again whether he could change my mind about continuing our date, but I stuck to my decision. He leaned in and gave me a very gentle kiss on the lips. He smelled like aftershave and toothpaste. Not a horrible combo.

CHAPTER 2

After law school, I moved to Washington, DC to work at a law firm on K Street. The next three years were a blur of long hours at the office, lectures from partners on the importance of "wordsmithing" a document and takeout dinners eaten with chopsticks with my computer screen as company.

The partners I worked for had no idea that at night, I was writing briefs and reviewing emails from the comforts of my group row house in Dupont Circle, a novel housing concept in Washington, DC for young professionals seeking affordable living space in an otherwise unaffordable neighborhood. With six wild roommates from all over the country, there were bong hits and keg stands going on downstairs while I was reviewing underwriting agreements upstairs. I shared a bathroom with a guy whose claim to fame was that as president of his fraternity he had once thrown a 100-keg party during his fifth year of college.

Our landlord eventually got fed up with the neighbors' complaints and the district's citations against us for various noise, trash and "drug odors." His first course of action was to send a letter by registered mail to each of our respective bosses, telling them what horrible specimens of human life we embodied and that we should certainly be fired.

The letter referring to me was addressed to the Managing Partner of my new law firm. It arrived the very first week that I started work. I had only lived in the house for 72 hours at that point, but the damage done by my new roommates before I arrived had already started to creep into my professional life. Everyone told me that reputation is everything as a first-year associate at a law firm. Nobody told me that this could be wiped out in an instant when your landlord goes off the deep end. Luckily, the Managing Partner at my law firm, Mr. Blad, was understanding. He introduced himself, explained that he had received a letter from my landlord and highlighted some choice phrases the landlord used to describe the reasons I should be fired. I can still feel the redness creeping up in my face when the following words came out of his mouth:

"Your employee is most likely a drug user or seller and someone like that is not fit for a job at your law firm or in the legal profession."

As I contemplated what my next career move would be, Mr. Blad advised me to "take care of this." He handed me the letter and walked out.

My law school torts professor once warned me that single female lawyers had to choose between having a love life and being an associate at a law firm. I think she mentioned this while going through a divorce, but still—this statement scared the hell out of me. Everyone around me was moving in with his or her significant other, planning a wedding or already married. As a single female in my late 20s, I was hoping that the constant parties at my group house would give me a leg up on my professor's rule of thumb. While I had built-in opportunities to meet numerous potential prospects, the guys that I met did not want girlfriends. In fact, the majority of single men in their mid-20s, living in a semi-urban environment like Washington DC, did not seem to have any real motivation or intention of settling down just yet. It meant that I was often disappointed and a tad lonely, but at least my constant companion, Work, and several close female associate lawyers at my law firm were always there for me.

After the plumbing exploded during my Dupont Circle house's glow-in-the-dark Spring Break party (my bathroom mate's orchestration), it was time to move. I found a great one-bedroom apartment two blocks away. In complete silence and without the distraction of a fog machine, ice luge or Tuesday afternoon beer funneling in the living room, I was free to fully commit myself to work.

By the time I had my fill of Washington law firm life and was looking to relocate back to New York City, my relationship with Brad had gotten serious. He was a welcome escape from third party subpoena requests for information and noncommittal, flirtatious guys.

After I left him on the sidewalk following our first date, he called five minutes later to ask what I was doing the following weekend.

"If I don't reserve you now, someone else might," he said.

During our first couple months of dating, there were plenty of romantic gestures. He used to pick me up at 9:00 or 10:00 PM from my office and drive me home, just to have fifteen minutes with me during my long workday.

On Valentine's Day, he walked two miles to my office in a complete downpour to deliver two dozen roses. The flowers came with a card containing instructions to meet him for dinner at 9:00 PM, knowing I would need to work until then.

Brad taught me how to starch a dress shirt, which he wore every day with a suit and tie to his banking job. He was driven, spontaneous and made me a soulful country music mix, a foreign concept for a Jewish New Yorker. He took me with him to get his car waxed every few weeks and enjoyed surprising me with reservations to five-star restaurants where politicians hung out. Brad's company was extremely welcomed at a time when my main social outlet was the law firm monthly luncheons to discuss billing efficiencies and all of my friends from college and law school were settling down with their significant others or were already married.

After a few weeks of dating, he accompanied me on a long weekend back to New York City to visit friends. Later on in our relationship, he told me that this was the trip where he fell in love with me.

"But what was the exact moment?" I'd ask him, delightfully anticipating the words that would follow.

"It must have been the taxi ride," he said. A grin took over his face and filled the tiny creases around his eyes. I had memorized those lines and how his smile made his blue eyes sparkle. Speaking about us was his favorite topic.

"On the way back from dinner?" I said.

He could barely get the words out, already laughing as he recalled the cab ride.

Now I was laughing, too. The moment we had gotten into the taxi, the out-of-place smell of a skunk was everywhere, covering us in the back seat. Why would it smell like a skunk in New York City? Had someone recently been sprayed and then decided to take a cab somewhere? Was the skunk still loose somewhere in the car? The smell was so strong that we briefly discussed finding another cab. It was raining, however, and we had already been trying to find one for ten minutes. We figured it was only a 15-minute ride at most and we could handle it. We rolled down the windows and tried airing it out. We tried breathing through our coats to block the smell, but it was no use. We fought to hold down our dinners until we arrived back to Brooklyn where we were staying.

We thankfully arrived in one piece and were grateful to be outside again, despite the rain. We walked a bit under an umbrella together to calm our queasiness. His arm was around my waist. We were still laughing about what we had just endured, holding each other tightly. He stopped me suddenly on the sidewalk and pulled me into his chest.

Tucking a dripping wet piece of hair behind my ear, he said, "Your friends are great. Tonight was fun, Stace. It's always fun with you."

He paused, looking down, fumbling for words. I wondered if I should say something.

"Are you falling in love with me?" he said. "'Cause I think I'm falling in love with you." Then that grin was there again.

It felt like the wind had been knocked out of me. Could it be love at this point? My brain began measuring out, like ingredients in a recipe, how love should feel. Did I have butterflies? Was he husband material? Could this be the guy I had been looking for? His upbeat energy was contagious. He was quick-witted, paid attention and said so many of the right things. Best of all, he wanted to call me his girlfriend.

Before I could verbally react to his falling in love declaration, he came in to give me a kiss. Within seconds, we stopped. The skunk smell had clung to our clothing. It was everywhere. He knew it and I knew it. We stared at each other for a second and exploded into a laughing fit.

"It's like we bathed in skunk juice," he said.

"It's everywhere. I think my eyelids smell. My hair, too. And my fingernails. Ugh, I must shower."

That 15-minute cab ride marked the start of our budding relationship turning serious. It didn't seem very romantic at the time, but picturing that foul-smelling taxi ride always made me smile. I may not have been able to openly declare my love for him at that exact second, but he certainly had potential.

It was an opportune time to fall hard for Brad, and fall hard I did. He was polished, spontaneous and had all sorts of ambitious plans for his life. He talked about going to business school, buying a big house out in California and settling down. He painted a picture of a life that I had been waiting for. Most importantly, I finally had a date to all of my friends' weddings.

CHAPTER 3

Brad's obsession with college football meant countless hours of game watching and learning about each of his alma mater's beloved players. We spent fall Saturdays parked in front of the TV, watching his team running up and down the field in grass stained mesh jerseys. My focus often drifted back to the sports fields and football fan attire worn back at Camp Echo Lake, a co-ed, eight-week overnight program in the Adirondack Mountains of upstate New York. I started going there the summer after fifth grade.

My fourth summer at Echo Lake, a new male camper arrived. His name was Jonny. My bunkmates and I used to watch this 14-year-old tall, lanky male play basketball in a faded Baltimore Orioles tank top for hours. We immediately declared him "adorable." At nighttime he'd switch to *Star Wars*-themed attire. This occasionally included a Darth Vader helmet saved for special evening activities. The only times he spoke to girls was when quoting *The Empire Strikes Back* during forced co-ed social interactions. He spent the rest of his summer with a hockey stick in his hands or running suicides on the basketball courts.

While hockey and basketball were the highlights of Jonny's summer, canteen was the highlight of mine. This was the hour after evening activity and before bed unofficially designated to helping hormone-ridden 13- and 14-year-olds work on their flirting skills while eating a pack of Oreos and drinking soda in the recreation hall. During canteen, Jonny would slip off to the lit-up basketball courts, more interested in a game of knockout or H.O.R.S.E. than thinking of clever things to say to a girl with potato chips in her braces.

I became a tennis staff member at Echo Lake the summer after graduating high school and began a relationship with Paul Fishman. Paul was a former bunkmate of Jonny's who I had admired from afar for several summers. We officially became a couple after kissing outside a Ben & Jerry's ice cream shop in Lake George Village the night before the campers arrived. He had an intense personality that came off as unintentionally quirky and amusing. Watching him play tennis was like witnessing a boxer in the most important match of his career. He grunted, he grimaced—he was all passion. He wasn't the chatty type unless lecturing a 12-year-old about the poetry of a Van Halen song. Half the time I had no idea if he was interested in me or found me too conventional for his taste, but when he returned a beautiful backhanded shot past his opponent with precision and authority, I was hooked.

Our relationship lasted a full two weeks, which in camp time meant it was very serious. After those two weeks, however, Paul dumped me for Softball Sarah, the new softball specialist at the camp. I was devastated. Mostly because I was head over heels for Paul and partially because I was a much better softball player than Softball Sarah and found it insulting that he'd chosen her.

Jonny was also on staff that summer. He managed the 14-year-old boys' group. By then, Jonny had started to come out of his shell and was filling out from his formerly skinny frame. We worked together constantly, ate three meals a day in the same mess hall and got to know each other fairly well. Snack time was 3:00 PM in the Grove every afternoon.

During one particular snack time at one particular picnic table, I was sitting with Jonny and several other staff members when I noticed an unfamiliar face sitting at the end of the table. It turned out that one of our evening program directors had a high school buddy visiting for the day. After being introduced to the pile of us sitting around the picnic table, the friend just sat quietly on his own, smiling at the stories we exchanged. His friend had gone off to flirt with someone, leaving the newcomer to fend for himself.

While the group chatter continued, I noticed Jonny go over to the guest and say, "Hey there, so how long you visiting for? And why on earth would you ever wear a New York Rangers hockey T-shirt?" I saw the visitor's face light up as he made some chitchat with Jonny, laughing at his jokes and defending his beloved hockey team. I was always amazed at how sports could become a universal language between total strangers. It seemed like a foreign language to me, but put two hard core sports fans together that have never met and they could spend hours analyzing their favorite teams' coaches, players, opponents, trades and actual performance during a game. Immediately, my respect for Jonny grew. He had the courtesy to break away from the comfort of our camp friends to make this person feel welcome. This small gesture exemplified how the kindness in people was either present or lacking, and with Jonny, how naturally being kind and inclusive had always been part of who he was.

At 18 years old, Jonny's attractive qualities continued to develop. His dark short hair and light blue eyes earned him the name "Superman," and his Clark Kent good looks did not go unnoticed. At the time, however, I still only had eyes for Paul.

A week after I got dumped for Softball Sarah, a group of us, including Jonny, spent a day off in Saratoga Springs, New York. We took three $40 motel rooms divided six ways and commenced playing innovative drinking games. By 3:00 AM, half the group was still competing while the other half wandered off to smoke joints or make out. I don't remember which group I fell into; however, I do remember waking up in a bed with Jonny and five other people scattered across the floor in the room.

In the early morning hours, Jonny and I shared our first kiss in that crowded, muggy Saratoga Springs motel room. It lasted about six minutes. Long enough to know that it wasn't an accident and short enough to prevent anything else from taking place. An hour later, as the group was headed for bagels, Jonny indicated that we needed to talk. Instantly, I knew our brief flirtation was over. After pulling me aside in the motel parking lot, he launched into a ten-minute speech about how much he liked me (as a friend), how great a person I was (in a platonic sense) and how he did not want to hurt my feelings (because he cared about me, as a friend, in a platonic sense), *etc.*

After the first 90 seconds of his speech, I couldn't help but smile. He looked so stressed. There weren't that many 18-year-old boys who could express themselves so openly. The latter part of his speech indicated that he was interested in another girl back in camp and hoped we could still be friends. I smiled and told him that no permanent damage had been done.

Jonny and I went straight back to being friends like nothing had ever happened. For the rest of the summer, I monitored Paul and Softball Sarah's relationship constantly and eventually my tireless devotion paid off. I got back together with Paul, who grew tired of Softball Sarah and had renewed interest in me. There was no evidence or conversations as to what suddenly made me so desirable again, but it didn't matter. We ended up dating on and off for the next five years.

This chasing of boys was a fun competitive sport in my younger years. The older I got, however, the less appeal it had, particularly with the noncommittal types.

After our Brooklyn trip, Brad and I took full advantage of doing what brand-new couples do. We called each other constantly with absolutely nothing of substance to say. We got excited about doing ordinary tasks together like folding laundry and competing for a parking spot in the crowded DC streets surrounding his home, We spent a weekend morning touring a new construction housing community, fantasizing about what it would be like to own a luxurious 4,500-square-foot monstrosity and put down roots together. He brought a new romantic element to my very limited social life that until then revolved exclusively around the law firm.

Brad never made me wonder how he felt about me. As soon as one date ended, he'd plan the next. After our Brooklyn trip and our decision to become exclusive, we flew to California to meet his parents. They welcomed me with a barbecue pool party they hosted for Brad's friends and lending us a car to hit up Knott's Berry Farm for the day. Brad won a gigantic stuffed Elmo doll for me by knocking down milk jars with baseballs. We dressed up at one of those old time photo places with the backdrop of a Western saloon. I was sitting on top of the bar with an off-the-shoulder, peach satin, poofy gown while Brad stood next to me in overalls, a leather vest, cowboy hat and a shotgun. Brad's mother hung one of the two 8×10 sepia photos we ordered on her refrigerator.

"When will you come visit us again?" she said when it was time for us to leave.

"Soon, I hope," I said.

"I haven't seen Brad this happy in a long time," she said, giving me a strong hug.

The feeling was mutual. During that time period, my colleagues at the law firm would constantly tell me that I was "glowing with happiness." It felt great to finally have an incentive to leave the office and something to look forward to after a long workday.

When I came home from work one day and found that Brad had cleaned and organized my entire kitchen and cooked me a dinner of Hungarian goulash, I knew that I had fallen for him.

"You are welcome to cook for me any time you'd like," I said. "I love this meal. And I love you too, you know."

CHAPTER 4

In the course of sending out feelers for new job opportunities to escape the law firm culture, I got word of an opening at Lehman Brothers in New York. It was a long shot, the job requiring several more years of experience than I had at the time, but the chance to go in-house and leave the law firm life behind was too enticing to pass up a try. The position was a chance to get hands-on business experience at a reputable and successful (at the time) company and would cut my hours in half. It would also allow me to return to New York, where my family and the majority of friends lived.

Once the "I love you's" were said, things moved quickly. Brad was luckily very willing to find a new banking job in New York City once I had settled in there. He moved in with me to a 400-square-foot studio apartment in Brooklyn Heights with one tiny window that faced the brownstones across the street. If you put your nose to the very bottom of the window and looked up at a certain angle, you could definitely see the sky. It was cramped quarters. We made our phone calls from the bathroom. Having visitors was impossible. Despite the cramped space, we made it work, spending weekends taking walks on the Promenade, having dinner on Montague Street and meeting up with my friends around New York City.

One of the greatest parts of being back in New York was the ability to attend a number of social events that I didn't have the time for at my law firm. One of these events was the annual fundraiser sponsored by Echo Lake for an affiliated nonprofit organization. Hosted at a venue in the Flatiron neighborhood of Manhattan, this was the first time in almost four years that I'd been able to attend a camp-related function. I was looking forward to introducing Brad to some of my oldest friends.

As Brad and I entered the club, I immediately recognized dozens of former camp friends, staff members and alumni filling up the event space. Paul Fishman was one of the first people to come over to greet us. After introducing my ex-boyfriend to my current boyfriend and watching them immediately hit it off, I decided that drinks would be necessary and headed to the bar. It was there that my face lit up upon seeing Jonny and Sarason, another favorite camp friend, also waiting for a drink.

After college, Jonny and Sarason's Murray Hill apartment became a hub for many camp reunion gatherings, last-minute parties and a great release from law school stress. I always looked forward to it and knew it would be fun no matter what we did. The two of them lived together for several years along with Cooper, a third camp friend from the glory days. At one point, Jonny lived in the small galley kitchen of the apartment for a few hundred dollars a month—a bargain for Manhattan living. His underwear most likely resided in the cutlery drawer and his décor had a combined *Star Wars* and football theme, but it was all worth it for a chance to live in New York City.

One night, after a particularly lousy day of classes and stress, I was invited over to Jonny's apartment to hang out with him and Sarason, with the only plan being to order in Chinese food. To my delight, they answered the door wearing sports jackets and ties, declaring an impromptu, semi-formal cocktail hour in their living room. Handing me an extra sports coat twice my size and a martini glass, they poured me a pink beverage of some sort. We sang karaoke, watched movies and retold old camp stories. I still remember how my face would hurt from laughing after hanging out with these guys.

At that point, my feelings toward Jonny could be described as a chronic crush, beginning around that day in Saratoga and continuing for the next twelve years. It was not the kind of crush that kept me from being involved in other relationships or made it awkward when we were around each other. It was more of an ongoing, heated, completely unreciprocated, romantic admiration. If I was around him, I liked him. It was impossible not to be drawn to him. My on-again, off-again relationship with his former bunkmate Paul may have made things a bit too complicated. At least that's what I told myself.

When I was finally single, Jonny had a girlfriend. When Jonny was single, he wasn't interested. Despite those six minutes of early morning kissing back in Saratoga Springs, it was clear that he didn't think of me as girlfriend material. My law school friend once pulled Jonny aside during one particular drunk summer night out to inquire as to whether there was a shred of possibility that he was interested in anything more than a friendship with me.

He responded politely that he wasn't.

Jonny and I occasionally went to the movies together. Knowing that there was no chance of a romantic connection, our time together was effortless and carefree. He somehow convinced me to see an anniversary edition of *The Exorcist*, which terrorized me for weeks. At the Central Park Zoo, he made me cry in laughter at his imitation of the red-tushed baboons. During a trip to Blockheads' burritos, he told me about his improv comedy group. We also discussed my aspirations of ditching the whole law school thing and becoming a writer.

"You should just go for it," he'd tell me over nachos. "Life is short and aren't there already enough lawyers in the world? No offense."

"I don't really like lawyers, either," I said, "but how do people just go after what they really want to do *and* pay bills?"

"Well. I guess you just take a chance. You accept being a starving creative type for a while and you hang in there long enough for a little luck to take over," he said. "Nothing's guaranteed, though. That's why I buy lottery tickets."

"That sounds like a great retirement plan," I said. "I envy your ability to just go for it. That takes guts."

"I've heard you can be very lucky with your writing if you donate half your guacamole to me. Don't jinx your fate. Hand it over."

Jonny was the only guy I knew in Manhattan who was not in law school, becoming a doctor or wanted an MBA down the road. It was a complete turn-on.

Back at the fundraiser, I introduced Jonny and Sarason to Brad, who asked them where they worked. It was clear that Brad was impressed with Sarason's joint JD/MBA degree from an Ivy League university followed by various prestigious jobs at a large law firm and several Fortune 500 companies. When it was Jonny's turn to answer the "What do you do for a living?" question, he spoke about his auditions for various movie and commercial jobs while waiting tables at night. Brad nodded his head in silence and quickly turned back to Sarason with more questions.

For just a second, I caught Jonny's eye to issue a telepathic apology. Once Brad started talking shop, I immediately zoned out, as I'm sure Jonny had too. It didn't matter though as Jonny's adoring former campers had already swarmed him, eager to say hello to the legendary camp celebrity. We spent the rest of the evening sipping drinks in one of the club's booths with Paul Fishman and a handful of other friends. It seemed like a strange dream where multiple worlds of childhood and adulthood friends unexpectedly combine.

The first six months in New York flew by and the move had proved to be well worth it. I loved working at Lehman—the people, the new position and having nights and weekends free for the first time in three years were very welcome. I was grateful during the spring and summer to see daylight when I left the office. It felt a little strange at first with all of the newfound free time in my life.

My relationship with Brad was also going very well, despite his long-term plan of settling down in California. He continued to cook dinner for us, bought me expensive gifts for no reason and seemed content with life in New York. After dating for a little over a year and after three months of living together in New York, Brad proposed on the first day of a Caribbean cruise vacation. My immediate reaction when I walked into our cabin and saw streamers, champagne, roses and Brad down on one knee was a mix between excitement and heartburn. I shouldn't have been completely shocked—we had gone to look at engagement rings a couple of months earlier. Still, his 26-year-old self asking my 29-year-old self to be his wife without having had any serious discussions about marriage seemed sudden. Despite my immediate doubts, that weeklong cruise was the highlight of our relationship. We fantasized about planning a large, traditional ballroom wedding with a kickass band and a chocolate fondue dessert bar.

———————

I couldn't even enjoy the ring, however, as I had been experiencing multiple stomach episodes that resulted in 16-hour bouts of throwing up and abdominal pain. These occurrences happened every three or four months and always ended in an emergency room visit hooked up to a morphine drip and anti-vomit medication.

Months were spent at different doctors' offices doing every test known to mankind: stool sample studies, colonoscopies, drinking chalky beverages that would map my digestive system on a scan, swallowing a camera in pill form to take digital photos of my intestines, CT scans, urine sample collections and specialized blood work—I was a living, breathing pincushion/test tube doll that was examined from top to bottom, inside and out.

While my body was being interrogated, the wedding plans moved forward. Not too long after the engagement, we looked into getting a bigger place. We rented a one bedroom in Manhattan in a high-rise rental building. It was certainly pricey but had all the bells and whistles one could want in an apartment. Plus it gave us another year to make any major decisions about settling down somewhere. The building had an indoor pool on the 40th floor and a gym, which got Brad excited. The apartment had an extra half bathroom, which got me excited.

We spent the next couple of weeks in and out of department stores looking at furniture before deciding upon a traditional bedroom set with a mahogany colored sleigh bed. We picked out a two-tiered wooden coffee table that matched the dark brown entertainment center for the living room. We bought a desk that required assembling for the alcove space off the kitchen and an expandable dining room table with eight cushioned chairs. We laid down on about 35 mattresses before picking one. Brad had his heart set on an extremely expensive, high definition flat screen television. We already had a television and I didn't see the need to replace it. Brad said he would pay for it himself, which he did.

It was thrilling to wander through department stores hand in hand, discussing whether we wanted a beige or navy couch, to get leather or opt for synthetic material. I loved that my life was finally starting, that I was going to have a life partner, someone to love and grow old with. Registering for our wedding and picking out our fine china with an infrared device was another exciting rite of passage. At each store where we registered, we would be greeted with champagne and well wishes, provide our names and mailing addresses and be handed the equivalent of a wireless checkout scanner. All we had to do was aim the scanner at a barcode on the item we wanted around the store and it would be instantly added to our registry. This certainly helped in keeping Brad's interest since the experience instantly turned into a video game.

I saw Thanksgiving dinners hosted at our home with elegantly displayed silver napkin rings sitting delicately on place settings out of a Martha Stewart catalog. I didn't even know how to make a turkey, but the thought of hosting a big feast with a tastefully decorated dining room table was a thrilling concept, probably something I had picked up from watching Stove Top stuffing commercials.

A month after we moved in to the new apartment, the wedding plans went full steam ahead. August 25th would be the date, a little over a year away. Once the initial shock of the proposal wore off, I found myself swept up in the momentum of wedding planning. Being a bride was a new elite status that came with free gifts from department stores any time we registered and a constant, "Congratulations!" and huge smiles from any vendor we visited. The enthusiasm was contagious. I was just excited to be marrying someone that I loved. How incredible that we got to throw a huge party with all of our family and friends as a bonus?

We booked the venue, the photographer, and I found my wedding gown. Like so many other brides, it was the first dress I put on. We had waited nearly three months for our Kleinfeld's appointment to go wedding dress shopping. When I walked in and saw dozens of brides surrounded by dozens of doting family members and friends, I wondered if I had undershot the experience. My mother and Emory friend, Erika Reff (the "Reff") were the only ones with me. They were practical and honest. The three of us sat in silent fascination watching groups show up in matching bridal party velour hoodies with their names on them, large groups of family members that included everyone from grandparents to babies. We were assigned a bridal consultant and waited our turn.

At Emory, Reff lived across the hall from me in our freshman dormitory. The day we moved in, she lent me extension cords, which were a lifesaver as there was no way the TV would otherwise have reached the one power socket in the room. I didn't know it then, but those extension cords and the energy they provided could very much describe the kind of friend that Reff has always been to me. I could walk into her room at any given moment and tell her crazy, horrible things that were taking place around me. She was always calm. Always the voice of reason. She never panicked about anything—she just did whatever was needed, no judging, no nonsense. A person like this is essential to have on speed dial at all times. Reff is my extension cord. She's another limb of my body that has always given me just enough extra space to get where I need to go.

When I told the Kleinfeld's saleslady what my budget was (under $3,000, under $2,000 would be even better), she winced and disappeared into a tiny back closet in the enormous store that carried "past seasons' dresses." She encouraged me to browse the dresses on the main floor area and noted there was a Reem Acra trunk show going on that week and a discount if I decided to purchase one of this designer's dresses. My mother, Reff and I went to work. Since I was planning a traditional ballroom reception, I wanted an elegant, satin ball gown. The prices of the dresses on the main floor started at about $5,000. While looking through numerous styles, we watched other brides come out of dressing rooms to model their favorite choices in front of their extended families and groups. Their respective audiences were clapping, crying, hugging each other and offering words of choked emotion. My mother, Reff and I would temporarily pause our gown search to watch the commotion.

"This is insane," said Reff. "I mean, do these people realize they are shopping for an article of clothing?"

"I know. It's like they just won a car on a game show," I said. "Are we on a different planet?"

"OK, ladies, follow me, please," our saleslady said.

We followed her into the "Pauper Pity" closet of gowns. That's where I found it. It may have been hanging with hundreds of other dresses wrapped in a zip-up vacuum-sealed plastic hanging bag, but since the gown itself didn't know that it was from several seasons ago, I guessed nobody else would notice either. It was a strapless, ivory satin ball gown with a fitted bodice lined with intricate pearl and crystal beading. The full skirt had large pleats and the train of the dress was patterned with beads matching the bodice. I stood in front of the mirror that offered 180-degree views, watching my mother and Reff's reaction in the reflection. No words. No fussing. I could tell from their eyes that they approved but nobody wanted to act too excited in front of the pushy saleslady, who quickly brought over a matching ivory colored tulle floor-length veil with crystal beading on the edges to complete the look. She then excitedly announced that this was a past season Reem Acra dress and that the discount would apply if I bought it that day.

When we were left alone in the dressing room after trying on ten more dresses, my mother knew that I was still leaning toward the first dress.

"It looks great, Stacey," she said. "But don't let them pressure you into it. If you don't love it, we'll go somewhere else."

"I do love it," I said. "But it's expensive. Even though it came from the poor person's area, it's ridiculously overpriced."

"Everything wedding related is overpriced," she responded. "It's a conspiracy and there's no way around it."

With that, we let the saleswoman know we would take the dress. Her face lit up and she squealed in delight, immediately grabbing me for a long, drawn-out hug and an exaggerated kiss on the cheek before moving on to hug and kiss my mother and Reff. She told all of her sales associates around her that we had another happy customer and they gave her matching large grins and shouted enthusiastic congratulatory cheers at me as we made our way to the checkout area.

"Isn't it just AH-MAZE-ING when we've found THE ONE?" she said.

We signed a contract for the dress too. Who knew that clothing needed papers? Once the wedding gown was chosen, we moved on to the bridesmaid dresses.

Reff and my childhood friend Lauren accompanied me to the store. Since Lauren had been delivering love letters for me since 5th grade and I had been telling her about my crushes since at least nursery school, it seemed only appropriate for her to be a part of my big day. Particularly since I forced her to watch *Little House on the Prairie* with me hundreds of times and she took such good care of my blonde doll Mary and her brunette sister Laura—named after the Ingalls girls. I'm not sure how many little Jewish girls had a doll named Mary, but in the upstairs toy room,

Lauren faithfully and repeatedly helped me dress the dolls for the imaginary Walnut Grove church we took them to. Lauren and I also felt the need to change our own names while playing "Little House," so I always chose the name "Robin," the coolest 80s name ever while she always wanted to be "Stacey."

As we got older, Lauren's loyalty never wavered. There was the summer after 9th grade, when I went away for two weeks and came home to find out that one of my closest friends was dating my first love. Sure, he was not my boyfriend, but my feelings for him had never wavered and this was no secret to anyone who knew me. I was crushed. Lauren immediately declared this the most horrible thing a person could do to another and agreed to be angry at the friend for me for as long as I wanted. It didn't matter what the excuses, apologies or circumstances were. She was on my team. If I ever decide to launder money, become a serial killer or operate an underground prostitution ring, Lauren will be my confidante. My parents always said they were sure that Lauren and I would be friends for life. Thirty-two years later, they are still right.

We made an appointment at Adrienne's on Orchard Street in the Lower East Side. I was looking for something in the navy or royal blue family when a girl came out of the back dressing room wearing a beautiful, dusty pink, strapless, chiffon A-line gown. The bodice had soft pleats and an espresso colored thin ribbon tie belt at the natural waist. Lauren, Reff and I immediately approached and asked about the dress. It was a Jim Hjelm Occasions dress, and the color was called "spice." Lauren and Reff eagerly took turns trying on the dress. I heard them whispering in the changing room about how much they loved it and that it was actually a dress they could wear again. They wanted me to make my own decision, though, so they did not initially share this information with me. As soon as each came out wearing the dress, I knew our search was done. I did pick out a couple of hideous ones with big bows and loud colors for them to try on just to see their reaction, but they just smiled and agreed to get whatever I wanted. True friends. That Jim Hjelm dress was the easiest decision of the entire wedding planning process.

In addition to my sister, Lauren and Reff, all of whom I had been a bridesmaid for, Emily was the final member of my bridesmaid squad. Although Emily lived out of town, she was equally willing to go with whatever everyone else wanted. This didn't really surprise me as Emily had let me bring, as a date to her wedding, my bathroom-mate from Washington, DC who threw the 100-keg party. She had never even met the guy, but it was not a problem. Emily was also an Emory friend. If Reff is the Voice of Reason and Lauren is the Epitome of Loyalty, then Emily is the Honest Soul. She laughs at all my stories, is always the one to keep calling even if I forget to call back, and is one of those people who is just plain nice. I love these girls.

I joined wedding websites and had an instant new group of "August bride" friends in various wedding planning chat rooms to exchange information with on an hourly basis. Our apartment was inundated with email and brochures about upcoming wedding events. Getting married seemed like an exclusive club, almost entirely removed from what being married would actually mean. These websites made marriage seem like one big magical party. At any happy hour, phone conversation or social event, talking about the wedding seemed to be the only topic of choice. What were my wedding colors? How was I wearing my hair? Had I found the dress?

Brad settled in nicely to his new job in New York. He didn't have many friends in the city but seemed content enough to stay busy with his job, play Xbox 360 and follow his beloved UCLA football team's season. Perhaps because he didn't have many friends in New York, Brad seemed to have a lot of time on his hands after work. He would often be on the phone with college friends back in California, which seemed perfectly normal to me until I realized that one of these people was his ex-girlfriend from college.

"But she's engaged," Brad would say to me when I questioned why he would want to talk to her.

"Nobody that is happily engaged reappears in their ex-boyfriend's life for no reason," I responded.

"Well, she knows that I'm engaged," he said.

"Good, well, now that you're both so happy with other people and have talked enough to catch up, it's probably time to move on, right?" I said.

Despite my input, every now and then Brad's ex continued to call. He wasn't hiding the calls; in fact, he almost took pleasure in the way I'd roll my eyes when her name popped up on his cell phone while we were curled up together, watching a television show. Brad would laugh it off, but there was no doubt he knew that this situation was not normal.

When she called again at 3:00 AM one night, crying that her engagement had ended, the only one who wasn't surprised was me. Brad declared his innocence in the whole matter. He was only trying to be a good friend. He valued his friendships with previous girlfriends.

"Stop being so jealous," he'd say.

Knowing Brad the way I did, it was obvious his behavior stemmed from an immature desire to feel pursued. When directly questioned about it, he was perfectly aware that maintaining an ongoing relationship with an ex-girlfriend in any way was not really appropriate, particularly after she openly declared some "feelings" for him that still existed.

CHAPTER 5

After another stomach episode landed me in the hospital under observation for a week with a 91-year-old deaf and blind female roommate with severe digestive issues, we were getting closer to finding a diagnosis. Once discharged and awaiting lab test results, Brad convinced me that a weekend trip to UCLA to see his alma mater's homecoming football game was a much-needed getaway after my week of being poked and prodded. We bought last-minute tickets and packed our bags.

We were both exhausted from our early morning cross-country flight to California. Our itinerary was packed with long walks to see the sprawling campus.

"Can we stop for a minute?" I said.

"We just stopped a few minutes ago," he said. "Let me carry your backpack. You'll be fine."

"Can we take a taxi? A horse? Maybe an airplane?" I suggested.

No response.

His former fraternity house was hosting a homecoming barbecue and beer pong tournament for all of its alumni. We eventually made it there, my entire body sore by then. We spent three hours sitting on old dusty couches that smelled like sour beer. Not once did Brad mention our engagement or wedding to any of his friends.

Something in our relationship changed after that UCLA trip. I'm not sure if it was my unspoken resentment at being guilted into a whirlwind cross-country trip or if the excitement of the initial engagement just fizzled. Over the next few weeks, things seemed off. I would sometimes come home from work to find Brad in an irritable mood, complaining about the messy apartment or arguing with me about wanting to book another trip out West. Other times, he'd say nothing at all and these days worried me the most. Brad started going for long walks on his own "to think" after work.

"I need to clear my head. Been trying to figure out some work stuff," he said.

Then there was the night when he claimed to be out with work friends at a happy hour, ditching our dinner plans and stumbling home drunk after midnight after not answering his cell phone for the previous seven hours. Too embarrassed to call any of my friends to tell them about Brad's absence, I could feel my pulse getting faster with each unanswered phone call to Brad's cell phone. Wouldn't my friends just say what I was already thinking? Red flag behavior is rarely a false alarm.

When Brad returned from his night out, he lay down on the couch barely able to keep his eyes open.

"Where have you BEEN?" I demanded, feeling the anger swirl up into my head. "I tried calling and texting you a dozen times. We had dinner plans, remember? Why didn't you answer your phone or try to get in touch with me? I thought you were in a ditch somewhere."

"Why errrrr you suhhh-screaming?" he said. He was a mumbling mess. "Jusss calm down. You're being sooooooooo dramatic."

"Are you kidding me right now?" I said. "You've been unreachable for seven hours, you didn't feel the need to call and you have nothing to say about this?"

"I'm going to buhhhh-bed. We'll talk in the morning," he said.

He walked into our bedroom, shut the door and awoke the next day, profusely apologizing and claiming not to remember most of the night. There was never a reasonable excuse for why he didn't call or where he ended up. The softer side of me wanted to believe that he just had a few too many drinks. The savvier side knew that a happily engaged person doesn't disappear into the night for hours on end without getting in touch. Nothing good could be happening.

I continued to see my gastroenterologist about once a week after my stay in the hospital. He was quickly becoming my therapist as well. Another possible diagnosis for my mysterious stomach problems was a chronic issue involving my appendix. We made plans with a surgeon to remove it laparoscopically. Who knew that a patient could walk into a hospital in the morning, go under general anesthesia, have a body part removed through their belly button, and then walk out of the hospital a few hours later?

The appendectomy was in mid-November. The day after the procedure, recovering on the couch, Brad and I got into a discussion about Thanksgiving plans. We were supposed to fly back to California again and spend the holiday with his parents.

"I know you're recovering, Stace, but I was really looking forward to going home and seeing everyone."

"I hear you. I know how much you miss everyone. But your parents solved the problem for us," I said.

Brad's parents and sister agreed to come out to New York instead and do one big Thanksgiving dinner with my family since the doctor forbade me from traveling for at least two weeks post surgery.

"Well, what if you just stay here with your parents and I'll go back for the holiday? It'll be quick enough and then you can just take it easy."

"Are you serious? I mean, we're a joint unit now. It's Thanksgiving," I said.

"I know, but I miss the sunshine, the warmth and even the ocean," he responded.

"Look, I get it. You miss California. It's holy to you. But Brad, I just had surgery. I'm trying to get better. I can't physically go there. We will eventually. Your parents and your sister have already bought their tickets to come here. So why do you need to go there and leave me behind? You're my fiancé! Shouldn't engaged couples want to be together on Thanksgiving?" Then Brad said those magic words that triggered the next phase of my life:

"Maybe I'm not ready to get married."

CHAPTER 6

The words hung in midair, suspended between me, the couch, and Brad. I wondered for a second if I had heard him right. Maybe if I blinked a few times, I'd wake up and realize this was just a bad dream. But my insides knew better. In fact, they registered the implication of his words faster than my brain could, already flashing adrenaline to every cell in my body. I tried to appear calm, treating this situation similar to how I'd approach a rogue bee buzzing around the apartment. If I didn't move too quickly or show much emotion, it wouldn't bother me. It might even go away. Get all worked up, angry and start flailing arms and throwing things—it would sting you for sure.

"What do you mean?" I said casually, trying to use the same expression as if he told me he wanted to take up ice sculpting.

My reaction would make all the difference. Wouldn't it? Somehow, despite the grip on my stomach and my knowledge that a critical point of our relationship was coming to a head, I thought my best hope of getting things back on track had everything to do with my reaction. All I needed to do was be calm and logical. Of course he wasn't ready to get married. Who is really ever "ready" to get married?

"There are a lot of things I've been thinking about lately," he said. "And I want to be in California for Thanksgiving. It's not just my parents I want to see—it's my friends, too. And I'm fine going there on my own. But that doesn't mean that I don't love you. But maybe I'm not ready to get married. I don't know...forget I said anything..."

A thousand thoughts swirled through my head. Was he just having a bad day? Was he homesick? Was it selfish to expect him to stay with me on this holiday when he hadn't been back home in a while?

Wait a minute. What an asshole! How selfish of him to make me feel bad for something I can't control—I just had a body part removed and he's questioning whether he wants to get married? I had a momentary mental groan thinking of how my family would react to Brad's last few statements. Then I thought about having to tell everyone in my life that things hadn't worked out between us. And then there was the awful thought of being alone again. I couldn't let this happen. I *loved* him. This wasn't really happening, was it?

I don't remember getting off the couch at that point. I'm pretty sure Brad was asking me if I was OK. He could have sounded an air horn in my face at that point—it wouldn't have gotten my attention. I grabbed the keys sitting on the Lenox porcelain dish (an engagement gift from a family friend), found my phone, my coat and walked out the door. Safely away from the apartment, I started walking west on East 40th Street, taking comfort in the car honking, construction noises and distant fire trucks to drown out the thoughts in my head.

My fingers started dialing my older sister Wendy. She always knew what to do when the end of the world seemed evident. And wasn't this the end of the world? Growing up, Wendy and I always pictured our future love life as our favorite teenage romance movie, *Dirty Dancing*. We used to watch this movie several times a week on a friend's borrowed VHS tape even though it was rated R and our mother forbade anything in that category. We were five years apart, but nothing brought us closer than singing every word to the movie's soundtrack in the backseat of my mother's car and dreaming of our own rebellious, muscular bad boys to give us dance lessons.

When she answered, I could barely get the words out.

"What?!" she asked. "What happened?"

"Brad just said that he might not be ready to get married," I responded. I whispered it softly, slowly, in disbelief—afraid that if anyone around me heard what I was saying, it might be true. At the time, I was too shocked for tears. Too stubborn to give our recent conversation merit by getting emotional. For the next ten minutes, I stood out in front of an Au Bon Pain bakery while my big sister told me in no uncertain terms that my fiancé was the most immature schmuck she had ever met and this would be the best thing that ever happened to me. I instantly regretted calling her. Did she really think that *this* was the best thing that ever happened to me?

By letting my family in the loop, I had unleashed a serious chain reaction of unwavering, uninvited opinions. By the time I had returned to the apartment, Brad had called three of my friends, two of his friends and his parents. His parents then called my parents, and that had pretty much triggered a land mine of phone calls, comments, expressions of sympathy, questions and pretty much everything that I wasn't ready for and couldn't begin to deal with.

Brad apologized when I got back to the apartment.

"I'm just homesick and work's stressing me out. I didn't mean to upset you, Stace," he said, "You know I love you, right? I mean, you're 'The One.' I know *that*. It's just that I'm a little confused about getting married—*right now*. It's probably just normal pre-wedding jitters, right? It'll all be fine. Please stop looking at me like that. I promise you, we'll be fine."

I got very little sleep that night. I refused to return any phone calls, not ready to respond to questions that I didn't have answers for.

The next morning, Brad showered and walked out the door for work. I was home for the week, still recovering in the apartment from the removed appendix while Brad was at his office. I had a "This too shall pass" type email from my mother and Wendy had called and emailed every two hours with messages like, "Stace, it's me. Are you alive? He's still a schmuck. Please call your sister."

My father, a man of action, drove down into New York City and walked into my apartment with a handful of written notes from his work spiral notebook. I knew I was in for a memorable lecture. To most human beings, a person who appears uninvited at their apartment doorstep begging to come in and share their opinion of your sinking relationship might not be tolerated. His showing up less than 24 hours after the "I'm not ready to get married" incident is not a surprising move. My father has never been one to conceal his feelings on any subject matter. It had gotten him into trouble more than once. I couldn't be upset with him for barging in to give me relationship advice, especially knowing that he has absolutely no mechanism for self-control. He is not one to sugarcoat. He calls it like he sees it and finds it astonishing that I am able to keep a clear head under circumstances like this. I have definitely inherited the calm-under-fire gene from my mother.

Once I let him in, I walked straight back to the bedroom and jumped into bed. There didn't seem to be much of a point in getting up that day. The whole world suddenly became exhausting, and doing anything other than lying in bed feeling sorry for myself seemed unnecessary. My father marched into the bedroom and started arranging the pages of his notebook, flipping back and forth to see where the best place to start was. He looked like he had been mentally preparing this speech for centuries. His hair stood out in all directions and it looked like he had been up all night too. I'm sure he was, talking my mother's ear off. It made me anxious to think about all the energy being used up talking about Brad and me. Snippets of frustrated conversation being shot back between my parents like a ping pong match. *What does she see in him? Why can't she just end it? Can I just go there now and force her to come back with us?* His fingers were slightly trembling as he held the notebook close to his chest. I could see that the agony in his eyes matched the pain that radiated in every cell of my body. He started reading from the notebook, which I immediately found distracting.

"Stacey, I am here on behalf of your mother and your sister. We've talked this over nonstop for the past 15 hours and have come to the same conclusion: This is the best thing that could ever have happened to you."

There it was. That meaningless expression again. Why did people insist on making such an insensitive, grossly untrue statement? I understood where it was coming from, but even if Brad and I couldn't work things out and I went on to find someone else and be completely content (a farfetched concept at the moment), how could Brad's actions over the last 24 hours constitute anything remotely positive? Certainly this might be something that I would come to realize in time. I sat there, fighting back the tears. Already missing Brad. Feeling all too sharply the emptiness of the bed next to me. How did it come to this? My father reading me handwritten quotes from himself, my mother and my sister on why Brad and I should end things? Did they realize they were talking about my future husband? Their son-in-law? The guy who would give them more grandchildren?

"I'd also like to say," my father continued, "that, well, although this all probably seems like a shock to you, that I have known for a very long time that this was never going to work out."

For the next fifteen minutes, my father proceeded to read a list of reasons why my fiancé and I were not a match made in heaven, why going on to marry Brad would be the biggest mistake of my life and how Brad was light years beneath someone I deserve to marry.

I was still his baby daughter. Wasn't it in his DNA to think these things about a guy that was breaking my heart?

When my father uses my name to start every sentence, he's got his mind made up about something and he won't stop repeating it until the message is delivered: "Stacey, you need to listen to me. Stacey, he's an imbecile. Stacey, the guy can't make a decision to save his life. He's not even close to being in the same category of mature as you. Stacey, have you asked the Reff about him? I mean, have you ever gotten an honest opinion of what she thinks of him? If you don't believe me, your mother and your sister, ask your friends!"

He also continued to comment that I should end this engagement immediately without looking back. He wanted to help me pack up my stuff and take me back to their house, the house I grew up in, that very second. In fact, I'm pretty sure that if I had moved in with him and my mother right then and there, they thought it would be like it was in the old days. Softball catches and batting practice on the front lawn, games of Sorry! and Monopoly every night after work, my father driving me to work (instead of school) and handing me a brown paper bag filled with a mom-made lunch. At times, I found that my father believed that having his almost 30-year-old daughter move back in with him and my mother was not only a suitable arrangement, it was a much better alternative to living on my own in the dangerous, outrageously overpriced, traffic-filled streets of New York City.

"Howard," I began, utilizing his first name when he's driven me sufficiently crazy, "your opinion is noted. I will never have to question what you think of Brad or my relationship."

"Stacey, you need to listen to me..."

"Howard, let me talk," I cut him off. "This is going to take some time to figure out. At least more than 24 hours and you need to understand that we have not broken up. We're working on things. You may hate Brad, but he's still my fiancé. I'm not an idiot. I just need some time."

"Stacey, there's no thinking necessary here. There is only one thing to do. End it and be done."

I gave him my best pre-teen eye roll.

"I'm telling you, Wendy, I mean Stacey—there's only one right thing to do. I may not know a lot of things, but I'm telling you this and it's what has to happen—move on and move on now. You need to listen to what I'm saying. I'm right about this."

My father left and Brad eventually returned from work. We talked again about what led him to being confused. Why he didn't give us a chance to even talk about it before he started calling people. It was immature, impulsive behavior. How had the boy who was so excited to move to New York for me, asked me to marry him and live in 400 square feet with me become the same person that was confused about spending his life with me? Was it the idea of marriage that confused him? Or was it me? Would more time provide him the comfort that was needed? Or was this just delaying the inevitable that something between us was broken and no amount of time or self-reflection could fix it?

His parents had gotten on the plane bound to New York for Thanksgiving, but I already knew that Brad was no longer welcomed at my parents' house for the holiday. Speaking of Thanksgiving, that particular one goes down as the worst one of all time.

My mother drove into New York City to pick me up and I met her downstairs while Brad awaited the arrival of his parents and sister. We drove the 45 minutes to my parents' house in the suburbs in silence, my mom already sensing how much pain I was in and knowing better than to engage me about ending things with Brad. Unlike my father and sister who were ecstatic that things were falling apart between us, my mother was a bit more sympathetic.

"I just want you to be happy," she said while facing a cold gray sky and leafless trees lining the Palisades Parkway. "I hate seeing you like this."

"I'm working on it, Ma," I said, turning on the radio to block out the thoughts in my head. A slow, weepy Survivor tune came on the radio and I immediately changed it to something more upbeat. Why were there always love songs on during a relationship crisis?

"You know, Stacey, there are other fish in the sea," my mother said.

"Why does everyone say that?" I asked. "I don't need a new fish. I like the fish I have. We're just working some things out."

"Uh-huh," she said. "Well, it shouldn't be that difficult. He has the chance to marry a girl like you and there's any trace of doubt in his mind? He doesn't sound very smart," she said.

"Can we talk about something else?" I said.

Within 30 minutes of being at my parents' house, I managed to get into a tremendous fight with my father. I had just sat down to catch the end of the Macy's Thanksgiving Parade on TV when he entered the family room.

"Did you end it yet?" he began.

"Hello to you, too. Can you please leave me alone? I'm not talking about this anymore," I responded.

"Stacey, listen to me. Get rid of him."

"Do you think it's that easy to just snap your fingers and end an engagement?" I asked. "A week ago, we were booking our honeymoon flights. Looking at wedding bands. Not to mention that I love him. Can you stop?"

My father's face got red as I mentioned the "love" word. He couldn't understand how I still possibly had real feelings for such a person.

"How can you love someone like that? It's *ridiculous*. You should thank your lucky stars that you didn't get married and have kids with this person. Also, you should change the locks on the apartment," he said.

"Howard, leave her alone," my mother chimed in. "She's a smart girl, she'll figure it out. Stop driving her crazy."

"She's not being smart about this. I am entitled to an opinion. Especially when it's the *right* one. *Your sister* and I both feel the same way."

My mother rolled her eyes. I turned back to see Santa Claus pulling up in his sled and dressed-up elves finishing off the parade while my father walked off into his home office, where he remained for the rest of the afternoon.

We never sat down to a meal of any sort. My mother had stayed busy through our cold war by cooking a turkey, making stuffing, a salad, probably hoping that we could eat our way out of the silence. Not feeling very thankful on that particular day, neither my father nor I stayed at the table for more than a few minutes. I refused to sit down when he was there and vice versa. A mature crowd we were not.

On the trip back to New York City, I told my mother that she needed to control her husband.

"Oh Stace," she said. "You know that's not possible."

When I put the key in my apartment door, I could already smell the familiar, comforting smells of Thanksgiving from the hallway. Brad's parents and sister had taken over our kitchen. They created a last minute feast including all of the trimmings. If I had thought about it more, I would have set up tape recording devices in the apartment before I left just to hear what had been discussed. Truthfully, I'm not sure it would have been anything that I wanted to hear. Brad greeted me warmly, with a long hard hug and a kiss. He took my hand and wouldn't let it go throughout the entire night.

"I love you," he whispered, sitting at our dining room table, his family around us, the smell of sweet potatoes and a pecan pie in the oven filling the air.

I barely spoke as he filled up my plate and was either rubbing my back or talking to fill the silence that permeated the entire meal.

While the meal was filled with those familiar wonderful, comforting smells and foods that had made up an entire lifetime of Thanksgivings, I had never felt so empty. It was a complete charade. His mother gave me a sympathetic smile whenever I looked remotely in her direction. His father made small talk and his sister, fully appreciating the awkwardness of the situation as much as I did, said nothing at all. When dinner was over and the future "ex in-laws to be" had gone back to their hotel, we lay on the couch and watched TV.

"I missed you so much today," he said. " I am so sorry for what I said. So sorry. I'm an idiot. I love you."

"Why would you say that you're not ready to get married then?" I asked, feeling like the "I love you's" from him seemed more and more desperate.

"I was confused. I've just been feeling overwhelmed with everything. But not having you in my life is not an option. I love you and want to spend my life with you," he said.

"This shouldn't be that confusing," I said, repeating my mother's words. "You're all over the place and it scares the hell out of me. You need to figure this out."

Brad was going away for work for the majority of December and I demanded that he use that time to think about what he wanted.

We discussed his finding his own apartment in New York in the meantime, even living on his own when he got back from the work trip to clear his head. Over the next week, he'd send me listings found online for people seeking roommates to get my opinion. As if having a vote on whether my fiancé moved out and where he would move to would make me feel more secure about our relationship. We ultimately decided that he would stay put for the moment. What would him moving out accomplish anyway? Would we start going out on dinner dates after work to see each other? Would we be staying the night at each other's apartments again? It seemed like we were going in the wrong direction.

Living together while determining whether your fiancé still wants to marry you is a bit tricky. How do you demonstrate to the person you're engaged to that you are in fact the woman of his dreams and that he should, of course, marry you? It became an exercise in dancing on eggshells. I found myself dressing better. Putting on higher heeled shoes, wearing more makeup and planning my outfits in advance so that Brad might suddenly realize that this woman living with him wore skirts and cute boots. I also made extra efforts at the gym because it seemed obvious that you would want to marry the skinnier, toned and better-dressed version of your fiancée. The clutter of mail that sent Brad into the occasional nosedive of a bad mood was regularly removed along with the dirty dishes in the sink. Despite all of these gestures, Brad still seemed confused. My father had not contacted me since Thanksgiving, only speaking to me through the occasional check-in email from my mother or a phone call from Wendy. He was not capable of discussing anything other than his loathing for Brad, unless asking whether the Jerk had moved out. My mother felt terrible that I felt terrible.

———————

When it was time for Brad's three-week work trip, I told him to take that time to think about what he really wanted once and for all. By the time he returned, I wanted to know—was he in or out?

Brad called me several times a day from his work trip, checking in to see who else had heard about our "situation" and what the reaction had been. He seemed oddly upbeat to hear about all of the feedback. On the second day of the trip, he told me that his boss was now in the loop on our relationship snafu. By the fifth day, Brad had been offered the opportunity to work out of their company's California office. Not that he was interested in doing this, of course.

By the time Brad returned to New York and the moment arrived when he would have his decision, my stomach was in knots. He had arranged to meet me at my office building at 1301 Avenue of the Americas at the outdoor entrance area. I kept looking for him to come sprinting past the pretzel vendor cart holding roses, panting, with tears running down his face just like Billy Crystal on New Year's Eve in the movie *When Harry Met Sally* to declare to Meg Ryan, "When you realize you want to spend the rest of your life with somebody, you want the rest of your life to start as soon as possible." So where was my Billy now? I saw Brad approaching. No roses, no panting, no tears.

When our eyes met, he gave me the big grin so familiar to me, the smile reserved just for me. He immediately wrapped his arms around me and placed a firm kiss on my mouth. For a moment, like the tragic runner-up contestant of every season of *The Bachelor*, I thought that everything would be OK. That some distance on the matter had kicked him back to the reality that his fiancée was still his best friend/soul mate/love of his life.

We sat down by the headless green-marble figurine fountain that I passed every day on the way into my office building. The setting was actually quite fitting for the occasion. An unrecognizable human that had lost its head. Brad told me about his trip, a couple of anecdotes from his work dinners, client meetings and conversations with colleagues. And then because there really was no other way to avoid it, I asked if he had a chance to think about his recent confusion about our relationship, about getting married. He immediately took my hand and squeezed it really tightly, looking down at it instead of at my face. "I love you so much," he said. "But I'm still confused about whether I'm ready to get married right now." No more words. So I filled in the blanks for him.

"If you're confused, we shouldn't be planning a wedding," I heard myself say.

I sounded so logical, because this *was* a logical conclusion to say in a situation like this. But I wanted to grab him, shake him, scream at him until his brain cells remembered just what a brilliant, special, beautiful and rational creature I was. I thought Brad would be relieved—I had agreed that our engagement had to end.

He was free. It was done—but he just looked sadder than ever.

The confusion, the self-doubt, the fact that my entire future was subject to his mental state *du jour*—it was not fair. I couldn't see it then. I loved this man. For all his faults and immaturity. For all the horrible ways he had handled our relationship, I still loved him. So when Brad whispered into my ear by that fountain where we ended our engagement that he still wanted to make things work, that he loved me, that he felt with a little more time, he would feel right about us getting married, I believed him. He talked about going to business school in New York and getting an MBA. About taking the GMATs, the business school entrance exam. *These* were the things holding him back from settling down right now. It was all the uncertainty about his career. His confusion had nothing to do with how he felt about *me*.

That night when we went to bed in the apartment we still lived in together despite no longer being engaged, he would repeat the "I love you's" again. Words that I wanted to hear but that seemed at odds with what he was about to do. Somehow through these words, spoken in whispers, he also informed me that the transfer to his company's California office had come through. He was moving back west. Through tears, I told him that I refused to visit him. That if he really thought this long distance thing was going to work, it was *he* who would have to make the effort. *He* would need to do the flying back and forth. He agreed to all of it, promising me anything that I needed to hear. I believed him to the point where I helped him pack up boxes.

Before he left, there was still one major thing that needed to happen. One of the most unfortunate parts of calling off an engagement is not just the love that's lost and the confusion that has arrived to live with you. It is making the wedding plans disappear. Canceling the wedding involved an impossible series of endless tasks. It should not be attempted alone. Thankfully, my family, who was secretly celebrating behind closed doors and private emails of virtual "high fives" with the Reff (and my other friends, no doubt), stepped in to help divide and conquer. The thought of calling up my wedding vendors that had sat down with us for hours to iron out the details of our upcoming event was too much to bear. My father dealt with the Hilton hotel, which kindly gave us our deposit back and canceled the contract. My mother called up Kleinfeld's to see about the dress. They were not nearly as forgiving. Not only did they keep our $1,000+ deposit, they sent us a bill for the balance of the dress. It didn't matter that it was still over eight months until the scheduled wedding date. Completely ignoring the canceled order, Kleinfeld's also left me a voicemail almost six months later informing me that the dress had come in and I should make an appointment for a fitting.

My sister had success explaining the situation with the photographer who canceled the contract so long as we notarized a cancellation letter and sent it back. Adrienne's, the bridesmaid dress store, kept the full deposits on all the dresses, no exceptions. Months later, Wendy told me that my family paid those deposits back to my bridesmaids.

The band, I took on myself. As soon as we notified the lady who had talked linen closets with us while selling us the perfect wedding band, she became an entirely different human, informing us matter-of-factly of the acceleration clause in the contract. The balance of the entire band's cost was due upfront. I then reached out to the head of the company by letter; he called me back. Once again, I had to discuss the entire situation of what had happened. The manager told me he had a daughter, hoped that nothing like that would ever happen to her, and then agreed to forgive the remaining balance. They still kept the $2,500 deposit for absolutely no reason, making it seem like they were doing me a favor even though they had more than enough time to re-book.

It's too bad all of those wedding vendor brochures and magazines do not include disclaimers that say, "Warning! Your fiancé may dump you without any reasonable explanation before the wedding. Make sure your vendor contracts have an out!" To be fair, it's unlikely that any cautionary counseling would have helped. At the time, I thought the most crucial factor of choosing a wedding band was making sure it had the versatility to play songs by Michael Jackson, Frank Sinatra and Tim McGraw. I didn't need to worry about our wedding being canceled—that only happened to unstable, dramatic individuals. The kind who appear on *Jerry Springer*. Who knew I'd turn out to be a *Jerry Springer* type?

Next came the negotiations with Brad on furniture, bills, our apartment lease and electronics. These discussions weren't pretty, but necessary. In the end, Brad agreed to pay his part of the next two months' rent, leaving me the balance of the lease to take all on my own in exchange for all of the furniture. He would take back everything that he came with—clothes, his beloved Xbox, some dishes and all of his football paraphernalia. The final item we negotiated was his ridiculously expensive, state-of-the-art, high-definition television that he had paid for himself. I didn't argue with him on anything else, but that television was mine. I considered it collateral for being dragged through the mud in a relationship gone awry. In a court of law, they would call this a reward for pain and suffering. Since you can't split a TV in half, someone had to keep it and it wasn't going to be him. I think my winning argument for the TV was that if things worked out like he said that they would, he would not really be giving me the television. I would just be holding on to it for safekeeping until we figured out a long-term plan.

As for the beautiful Tacori platinum engagement ring, the question of what I did with it seemed to be a very popular one after calling off the wedding. I suppose it was easier to ask about the ring instead of whether I felt like continuing to breathe at any given moment during those first few weeks after calling off the wedding.

There were multiple options for dealing with the ring's final resting place. I could have sold it and given the money to charity. I could have sold it and used the money to pay off the wedding vendors who wouldn't return our money. It could have been used to offset Brad's portion of the rent and some seriously needed spa treatments. There was the option of keeping it too, hoping to someday wear it again when we were back on track. But that would just have made me sad. Who needed to look at something from time to time and feel sad? In the end, I determined that the ring belonged to Brad. He bought it with money he earned and with help from his family. It wasn't his family's fault that Brad had ruined our engagement plans. So I gave it back.

The last week of December was Brad's final week in New York. He planned to drive home to live with his parents until he could find a new place out in California.

As the time approached for his departure, each day was filled with his declarations of love and promises to come visit. There were about 100 times a day when I knew this relationship was never going to recover, followed by 101 times when my hope that it could change won out. He bought me ridiculously overpriced presents for the holidays that year—a Coach handbag, a Tiffany's silver bracelet, a Gucci watch, and a package to a high-end spa. Reff called them my "consolation prizes" and later said that this guy didn't know me at all. She surmised that he had taken a trip down 5th Avenue after work during a particularly guilt ridden moment and went holiday shopping crazy on me. Come to think of it, Tiffany's, Gucci, Coach and the spa were all within a couple blocks of each other. At least he was efficient. But when had I ever been interested in fancy handbags or jewelry?

Later, I made a personal rule that all other traces of a former significant other must be removed from an apartment. This includes photos (why beat yourself up looking repeatedly at a picture of happier times that don't exist anymore?), T-shirts with your ex's alma mater on them, trinkets representing inside jokes. There was one exception to this rule, and that included luxury items, so long as they didn't have much of an emotional attachment when utilized. The flat screen television counted. So did the Gucci watch. The other stuff I wrapped up in pretty boxes from the dollar store and gave out as gifts, with full disclosure on where they had come from. I found that people were only too happy to rid me of these items.

One of our last nights together in New York before Brad's big move was New Year's Eve. We struggled over what to do for it. I was pretty sure that none of my friends would feel comfortable hanging out with us—we were an odd pair. We went for dinner at a seafood restaurant and talked about anything other than the fact that in 48 hours, my ex-fiancé/boyfriend would be moving out of our apartment and driving 3,000 miles away to a different time zone and life. After dinner, we watched the actual ball drop on the HD television that would soon be owned by me alone. Brad promised that the New Year would be a great one for us. Because all great years start with the person you love moving as far away from you as logistically possible.

We spent the next three days changing the utility bills over to my name, waiting in line at Sprint to split up our cell phone plan and killing time at the DMV before turning in his New York State license plates. Then it was moving day. The last suitcase had been packed and shoved into his freshly waxed Honda Civic trunk.

We embraced one last time as roommates, ex-fiancés about to embark on a long distance relationship. Was there any realistic possibility that we could be happy together again?

CHAPTER 7

The tears would not stop. And even as he pulled away, bound for the West Coast, the sadness continued for much of the next three months. I remember going back to my (not our) apartment, lying in bed and staying there for much of the next week. My parents and Wendy took care of informing relatives and some of my friends that the wedding was officially off, which led to more phone calls from people who wanted to see how I was doing.

"He was probably gay," one family member offered.

"He had to have been cheating on you," said a friend.

"It just wasn't meant to be," said everyone.

This would ultimately result in the difficult explanation that we were still trying to work things out. This latter part always sounded a bit forced, like I was pleading with people to believe that a happy ending was actually still possible for ex-fiancés.

After much hesitation, I started becoming one of those New Yorkers who saw a shrink. Paying someone to listen to your problems felt strange at first, but then I kind of opened up to it. Some days, it was a relief to know that there was a place I could go to where I didn't have to act like a civilized, professional person. Where I could say whatever I wanted. Still, there was something inauthentic about having to write a check at the end of each session. That even though I appreciated the ear, it was a "paid ear," like prostitution services for the mind. For that reason, I was adamant that my therapy would have a start and end date. That unless I started having a nervous breakdown, I would avoid taking any anxiety treatment drugs. These weren't made-up problems in my head. These were real issues causing me real sadness, and I wanted to think, write and talk my way out of them.

Going to work was the best thing that could have happened to me during those first dark days without Brad. The apartment had an empty feel to it, like it almost echoed with all of his stuff gone. I hated being home by myself but going anywhere did not help much. At least at work, I had endless amounts of tasks to fill my brain. Not only did I cry on the bus on the way to work, I cried in the bathroom at work. I cried going to lunch. Sometimes I'd cry while eating my lunch in the bathroom—particularly on days when I hadn't slept the night before and didn't want to run into anyone in the cafeteria or street who would accidentally ask me how the wedding plans were going. Seeing couples on the street holding hands would send me into a fresh set of tears. But I was a serious lawyer with a serious job and needed to wipe this stuff out of my life during working hours. No crying at the office—another rule! I decided it was better to inform people first before anyone started asking questions about why I wasn't wearing my engagement ring. I went into my boss's office and told him that there was some news he needed to know from me.

"Please tell me you're not resigning," he said.

"No, no—it's not that," I responded.

I then proceeded to tell him in the quickest and most matter-of-fact state possible that Brad and I had called off our wedding and he had moved back to California. I pretended that I was talking about the status of an ominous work project. I used the format of: *This is what happened, this is how I'm dealing with it. Let's move on with our day.* It helped to pretend that I was reporting on somebody else's life and not my own confusing and stress-induced one. I ended the conversation with a reassurance that I was grateful for my job to come to every day and actually requested that any additional assignments or work that needed doing be routed in my direction.

"Bury me with work," I said. "I don't want time to think about anything else." I had similar conversations with several other close colleagues of mine in the office, letting the news trickle out from them. Finally, I felt like I could breathe at work again—the news was out, people could make of it what they wanted. So I wasn't just the happy-go-lucky, hard-working, straight-arrow lawyer girl. I was also a person who called off weddings and had unstable relationships with fiancés. So be it.

Gradually, I got into a routine. Wake up, remember he was gone. Cry or feel sad. Get in the shower. Cry in the shower. Sing sad love songs about breakups in the shower. Get dressed. Feel sorry for myself while drying my hair. Then worry it looked like I had been crying on my way to work. Become instantly irritated at anything happy around me on my way to work. Pass and be jealous of a five-year-old on Sixth Avenue walking around with her parents, her only thought in life being how happy she was to be holding a hot pretzel from a street vendor. Get to work and bury myself in the endless amounts of emails that had come in since the night before. Leave work and most likely fight back a tear or two on the way home. Go to the gym. Fight urge to leave gym if there was a rush hour line for the treadmills. Run 30 minutes on treadmill while kind of checking out every single male who walked by, wondering how on earth people met each other and stayed in love long enough to get married. Go home. Return incessant phone calls from my family making sure I was still alive. Wait for him to call. Talk for five minutes if he did call, often arguing about some mundane detail such as when the next time we would see each other would be or the invitation for sushi dinner by a new female neighbor in his new apartment complex because he had helped her move boxes into her new place. How generous of him.

Still, Brad made good on his promise to come visit me regularly, proving that he was somewhat serious about continuing to make things work between us. Just what we were working on was not very clear. Dating one's ex-fiancé is a very delicate endeavor, not to be attempted by the feeble hearted or sane. There is a good reason why calling off a wedding often does and should mean the end of the relationship. It is difficult to go backwards with all of the planning, expectations and advancements that had already taken place as an engaged couple.

That gray area of daters turned fiancés turned back to daters was far more painful than the problems leading up to the broken engagement. Life was on hold. I couldn't talk to my family about it—they just couldn't understand the rationale for continuing to be involved with Brad.

I'm not a regular crier, but I cried more during those months than in any period of my life. I couldn't go to weddings for several months. That just seemed like a complete impossibility given the circumstances. I missed the wedding of one of my oldest friends, but she completely understood and never took it personally. Witnessing any bride's beautiful moment filled with love and hope and whispered inside jokes with her groom—who actually showed up to the wedding and was equally excited to marry his bride—was not something I could endure at the time. Not only had this very image been taken away from me, but there wasn't much hope of finding my own happy ending anytime soon.

While my undefined, barely tolerable relationship continued on thin ice, the quest to determine what was causing my stomach episodes also continued in full force. I remember going to my doctor's office one afternoon, sitting in his private office and bursting into tears when he asked me where Brad was. When you're sitting in your gastroenterologist's office because of severe stomach episodes but the most pressing ailment is your current ex-fiancé/boyfriend, it's time to reevaluate the relationship.

In mid-April, I bit the bullet and took my first and only trip out to California since Brad moved there the first week of January. The entire weekend, I had this gradual sinking feeling in my gut about us but couldn't point to anything in particular triggering it. Brad was as nice as ever, repeatedly reaffirming his love for me, his belief that it would all work out and his plans for us to live together in California in the near future.

It wasn't until I was flying back to New York after that visit that I knew it was over. A rare moment of clarity. There was no specific reason that I could give to my friends for why I called up Brad the day after I got back and acknowledged that it was over. It had been more than three months since he moved to California and we were no closer to figuring out how to end up together. Perhaps I grew impatient. Perhaps there is a limit on brain cells being used up on over-analyzing a relationship with the same person. Perhaps I was sick of living phone call to phone call, waiting for someone else to figure out from 3,000 miles away that I was "The One."

"You take care of yourself, Baby," he said to me.

He didn't even sound too surprised or upset when I told him that it was over. I felt like a baby at the moment: born into a newly single, unfamiliar world where I'd need to relearn how to do everything.

When it was finally clear that ending our relationship was the right thing to do, I asked Brad not to contact me in any way for at least the next two weeks. He agreed. For the first couple of days, it was surprisingly not the end of the world. There was, if we're *really* being honest, the occasional thought that I was going to die alone, but I tried to stick to a formula of staying busy, making plans and looking forward.

My initial "freeze out" of Brad, which meant no calls, texts or emails lasted a full three days until I passed a guy on the street that I thought looked like Brad, was overwhelmed by how much I missed hearing his voice and gave in to calling him. We chatted on and off after that, mostly off, until I told him we really couldn't speak at all anymore. He missed me too, he said, but I had the feeling that he had already started to move on. He was no longer saying his insistent "I love you's" and his contact attempts had sharply fizzled.

Then two weeks after my trip to California, I got a phone call from Brad at 1:30 AM on a Wednesday night. He had been drinking a bit and started asking flirtatious questions like if I still missed him, if I thought about him a lot. I was about to tell him goodnight when he asked whether I was seeing anyone.

A bit taken aback, I responded, "Why would I be seeing anyone? We just ended things a couple weeks ago."

"Oh," he said. "Because I started seeing someone."

CHAPTER 8

Her name was Rebecca. She had studied to be a rabbi but was now leading a Hebrew educational program at a local Los Angeles-area synagogue. She kept kosher, went to temple on Friday nights and was now dating my ex-fiancé, a man who ate bacon for breakfast and had a Christmas tree. According to Brad, they started dating two weeks after we officially ended things after meeting at a Jewish singles event.

He had already met Rebecca's two sisters and her mom, and she had met his parents several times. Why I chose to listen to this information, I had no idea. He made sure to also reveal that the relationship with his rabbinical degreed girlfriend "had gotten serious." In those exact words. Well, as serious as a recently single man can get with another human being in two weeks, or however long they were really together before he told me.

It was not one of my finer moments, but after that phone call, I'm pretty sure Brad was clear on how I felt about him and his new relationship.

"Does this girl have any idea that she's involved with a lunatic?" I asked.

"Don't be mad," he said. "She knows about you. A couple of times I've accidentally called her Stacey. She doesn't like it."

"I can't listen to this. I'm literally becoming dumber. Good night," I said, and hung up.

It was pretty clear that there was absolutely no reason to have any more contact with him again. I removed his number from my cell phone, blocked him from all forms of communication and started thinking about what it would be like to start dating someone else, to call someone else my boyfriend. It didn't seem logical, but I knew that at some point, I would need to try.

Though heavy hearted after this definitive end, I had no doubt that it was the right move. And because I knew it was right, being in the apartment, *our* apartment, by myself felt different. When my sister heard the news, she was in her car within the hour, bringing large packing boxes and tape—probably grinning ear to ear the entire ride in and spreading the news to my parents.

"Let's do this!" she cheered when I opened my apartment door. She wasn't wearing a cheerleader outfit, but I knew that she'd been rooting for this particular moment with uncontrollable, enthusiastic patience.

She wheeled up the long cart from the lobby and stacked it five feet high with empty boxes.

It was time to get any and all reminders of Brad out of the apartment. We eliminated photo albums and framed pictures that I couldn't bear to cry over any longer. We chucked the stuffed Elmo, sweatshirts and T-shirts with the UCLA name, birthday and Valentine's Day cards, notes he had attached to flowers sent to my office and even dishes which Brad indicated he would come back for at some point. I made Wendy promise that certain things (like the cards and the photos where we looked happiest) were sent directly back to him. Why should I be the only one forced to look at the memories? The rest of the stuff she could do with as she wanted.

After Wendy left, I immediately began to rearrange the furniture and fill up the empty closet and drawer space with more of my own stuff. I started calling back all the people that had asked me to do things since hearing that Brad moved away. I was still sad of course, but if I examined my feelings as a pile of a million little pieces all scrambled inside my gut, I'd definitely describe a chunk of them as relief. Because the end was really never as bad as I feared it. It was finally my chance to start something new, to say goodbye to the worrying, confusion and self-doubt. For that, I was certainly ready.

There was just one last hurdle.

After undergoing an additional round of specialized blood work and scans, doctors finally discovered the cause of my stomach episodes: A carcinoid tumor was found in my small intestine, a rare type of slow-growing cancer. My family started making phone calls to find a surgeon familiar with this type of disease, and plans were made for its removal at Mt. Sinai Hospital. It was both a relief and a terror to have a diagnosis for the cause of these ongoing stomach issues. At the very least, it was a quick remedy for a broken heart. When your life's on the line, pining over an ex-fiancé quickly goes to the bottom of the priority list.

The date of my surgery was just a couple weeks away. An old camp friend dragged me to a fundraiser. I pretended to be a regular 30-year-old single girl out on the town. Jonny and Sarason were there. After a couple drinks, I told them about my broken engagement and upcoming surgery. They group-hugged me and promised to visit during my five-week recovery. Sarason said I should come to his wedding despite it being the same day mine was supposed to be. When he mentioned that Jonny was bringing his girlfriend, I felt sad and a strange tinge of jealousy. Being engaged had meant no more scrambling for a date, but my fiancé was gone.

CHAPTER 9

Two weeks later at Mt. Sinai Hospital, I was wheeled into a six-hour surgery. When they told me to count down for the anesthesia to kick in, my pulse pumped in fear—would I wake up again? Who would come to the funeral? Were there any other 30-year-olds who had called off a wedding and had life-saving surgery in the same year? The anesthesiologist told me to think of a calm, happy place, but what could that possibly be lately? He tells me to count backwards from ten.

"Think calm, happy thoughts," he says.

My eyes close. Ten, nine...

I am sitting on the couch in the family room next to Gretl von Trapp watching our favorite movie for the 165th time. The hills ARE alive and there is Julie Andrews running through the green mountains of Austria, singing at the top of her lungs. Then it's on to the nunnery where we ponder how one might solve the problem of Maria. We watch the Reverend Mother telling young Maria about the "family out in Salzburg who needs a governess until September to take care of seven children." We hear Maria's protests. "Don't worry, Maria," I whisper. "When God closes a door, somewhere he opens a window."

Uncontrollably, my foot starts tapping, particularly, the first night Maria spends at Captain Von Trapp's enormous estate and the rebellious 16-year-old Liesl sneaks out to meet her Nazi telegram-delivering boyfriend Rolf for some dancing in a glass gazebo, a song and a kiss. It is magical. Suddenly, there's a thunderstorm, a song about favorite things and before we know it, Maria is cutting up curtains and turning them into play clothes. Gretl and I are learning how to sing in the mountains of Salzburg while running through Mirabell Gardens. We climb trees, fall out of a boat and meet the meddlesome Baroness Schräder. After the von Trapps happily escape by foot to Switzerland, Gretl and I applaud the conclusion, feeling replenished. It's the equivalent of a vacation for a six-year-old and her doll.

The surgery was successful—the tumor and various surrounding body parts were removed, my gallbladder among the sacrificed. I'd soon receive monthly injections that caused gallstones as a side effect—the purpose of its removal. Peering inside my gown, metal staples and black string were stitched into a gaping linear wound that extended from below my breasts to two inches under my belly button.

Seven days later, I was discharged and the nurse unstitched tubing from my neck. I did a double take as I saw Jonny in a commercial on the hospital room's television hanging from the ceiling. He was sitting on a park bench, chatting with Ronald McDonald.

"Ma!" I said, "Look up! It's my camp friend on TV!"

"Is he the cute, tall guy or is he Ronald?" she joked. "He kind of looks like Clark Kent."

Was this a sign? The nurse applied a bandage to my neck and I was officially free. Forms signed, luggage packed—I was ready to go. This was it. My entire body was free of tubes, wires and medication. I walked out of the hospital and braced for the new life ahead of me.

CHAPTER 10

Jonny made good on his promise to come visit after the surgery. In fact, he was one of my earliest visitors. When he called to see when would be a good time to come over and what he could bring, I reminded him about the liquid diet and that if he brought anything that looked, smelled or tasted good, I would have to kick him out. Instead, he showed up with ice pops and gave me a gentle hug. Immediately, an unfamiliar nervousness came over me as I struggled to be glamorous in pajama pants and a T-shirt.

"Here's the deal," I said, giving him a hug at the front door. "You can't make me laugh, because it really hurts whenever I do, so don't say anything funny."

"But *everything* I say is funny. I might as well leave now," he responded.

We sat on the couch, making a toast with our ice pops and caught up on the last five years of our lives. We realized that there was a lot about each other that we never knew. I learned that Jonny had fallen in love with New York City, despite being from the Washington, DC area, that he was obsessed with fantasy football, the Washington Capitals' ice hockey team and saw about one or two movies a week at the movie theater. He learned that I had played softball in college, that even though I was a corporate lawyer, I was still interested in pursuing a writing career full time and that I had an exceptional natural talent for the Ms. Pac-Man video game.

For almost two hours, we jumped from topic to topic—a conversation about ping pong leading to an analogy about a scene from *Star Wars*, which then somehow turned into discussing the dogs we had grown up with and the sports we played in high school. As easy as our catching up flowed back and forth between us, it came to a grinding halt when I ask him the following:

"So what's going on with your girlfriend? You guys have been together now for over a year now, Sarason told me. Do you think she's 'The One'?"

He paused for a few seconds.

"Yeah. Well, I kind of feel like…well, in some ways…umm, part of me is a little…."

More stammering. A few more half-sentences. Then finally, Jonny's familiar smile came back and lit up the room.

"Does that answer your question?" he said.

I winced in pain since his last question made me chuckle a bit. Jonny told me about the last 14 months of his current relationship. How they met, why he was attracted to her initially and then eventually, some of the reasons why he didn't see it going anywhere though he cared a great deal for her. He changed the topic and asked me about Brad. At what point I knew that it was over. He reminded me that he had shown up to my impromptu engagement happy hour the week after our cruise where we got engaged. It was so last minute that many people couldn't come and Brad and I ended up leaving before Jonny and Sarason got there.

I told Jonny how things had ended with Brad and how I had been dealing with it all. The subject of Sarason's wedding came up.

"Well, now you can go!" he said. "It's going to be a blast."

"I'm sure it will be. But there's a 0% chance that I'll want to travel to St. Paul, Minnesota to attend a wedding on the same day that I was supposed to get married," I started.

"Oh come on," said Jonny. "You can't miss Sarason, Cooper and I doing our wedding version of our Michael Jackson 'Thriller' dance. You'll be so terrified, it will be impossible to think about anything else."

"I'm sure that's true," I said. "I'll think about it."

It was a lie. There was no way that I was going to that wedding. It would be too emotional, too difficult and I hoped to be surrounded by family and close friends on that day. Attending someone else's wedding, no matter how much I loved Sarason, would not really be a distraction from the canceled wedding where I was playing the role of bride.

As I was escorting Jonny out the door, I half jokingly said to him,

"Well, if I somehow get the urge to attend a wedding that weekend and you break up with your girlfriend, we can be each other's dates. Hopefully by then, I'll be able to laugh again."

"Interesting idea," he said.

He promised to return with Sarason a couple weeks later to check up on me. Which he did. They brought over an adult version of the Mad Libs game, and we entertained ourselves for hours coming up with inappropriate, immature, X-rated adverbs and adjectives. The laughing hurt a little less that time. I received more pressure to attend Sarason's wedding, though my sensitivity surrounding that weekend was understood.

CHAPTER 11

My postsurgical liquid diet, a low dose of chemotherapy pills and having three and a half feet less of intestine did wonders in terms of dropping a few extra pounds. I went from a Size 8 to a Size 2 in six weeks. I'm pretty sure you won't see any infomercials on achieving this the way I did. With 20 pounds less of me walking around, I felt like a whole new person. Slowly but surely, I started exercising again. First came the long walks, then a slow jog mixed with a run. The exercise was a great way to counteract the effects of the chemo pills, at least when I wasn't nauseous. Before I knew it, I was back into the swing of things.

When the email came that night, I almost deleted it. Cooper—another male camp friend and former roommate of Jonny and Sarason—and I didn't speak regularly, so I did not recognize the email address. What caught my attention was the subject line which said "Sarason's Wedding." It read:

Stacey,

I hope you are feeling well these days. Are you going to Sarason's wedding? I'm flying out to St. Paul on Friday afternoon, August 24th, for the rehearsal dinner and made my return flight for Sunday. Turns out I get a date to this thing. So if you want to book a flight—it will be a great weekend. I'm planning to crash with a buddy but you're welcome to join. Let me know what you think.

    Cooper

It's funny how a quick, simple email can set the wheels in motion for major life-changing events. I read and re-read this email several times, trying to understand what Cooper was saying. Was this an invite to be his date at the wedding? Or was he just generally letting me know that he was invited with a date and thought it might be fun to hang out at the wedding with our other camp friends? If I did go as his date, this would definitely be a platonic invite, considering there was an unknown third party staying with us. Was I comfortable with that? I could go, be his date and get my own hotel room. But the prospect of spending my would-be wedding night alone in a room in a strange city seemed less than appealing. I pictured myself crying into the king-sized down pillows of the hotel room and sobbing during the ceremony, passing it off as tears of joy. Cooper was a nice enough guy, but there was only one person that I thought might have a shot at keeping my mind off of what wasn't happening that weekend.

I hit the "forward" button on my keyboard and sent the following email:

Jonny,

What do you make of the below email from Cooper? Being his former roommate, I figured you might be able to translate it. Is this an invite to be his date? General information on Cooper's itinerary for Sarason's wedding? Or an attempt at haiku poetry? If you can solve this puzzle, I declare you Smartest Man Alive.

Stacey

PS

Did you break up with your girlfriend yet so we can just go to this thing together and I can avoid an awkward rejection response to Cooper?

PPS

Just kidding about the girlfriend breakup thing. Well kind of.

After pressing send, I started pacing around my apartment. Would Jonny respond? Would he be offended that I told him to end things with his girlfriend? What would going to this wedding actually be like?

Five minutes after I pressed "send" on Jonny's email, my cell phone rang and it was him. Adrenaline instantly flashed through my body.

"Hello there," said Jonny. "I got your email."

"Oh good," I said. I felt my face getting red. "Wasn't sure what that email was all about. Figured you'd be a good person to ask."

Over the next few minutes, I listened in stunned silence as Jonny indicated that he actually *had* been considering ending things with his girlfriend over the last several weeks. At the moment, she was in Italy on a two-week trip and he felt that to officially end it, he owed her an explanation in person. That said, he told me not to respond to Cooper, because he, Jonny, would be needing a date and between my apprehensions about the weekend and him feeling down about his breakup, we could console and distract each other *and* have a good time.

"I have no idea what Cooper's email meant, but don't worry about it. You're going to that wedding with me. I'll deal with Cooper," he said. "Leave this with me."

"I'm not even sure I want to go to a wedding that weekend," I said.

"Well, I've made the decision for you. You're going," said Jonny. "Start looking at flights."

And that was that. Within 48 hours, flights were booked and I left the hotel-room and breaking-up-with-his-girlfriend bits to Jonny.

A week later in early August, four of my Emory girlfriends and I went to Rehoboth Beach in Delaware for the weekend. It was a whirlwind weekend filled with sunning ourselves on the beach during the day, walking the boardwalk and having sundress attired dance parties in our hotel room at night. On Saturday late afternoon, when everyone was showering and hanging out on the balcony of our room, Jonny called. He sounded distraught. His girlfriend had returned from Italy and he had ended things. Only she did not see the breakup coming and was very upset by the whole thing, making Jonny feel even worse than he already did. Being the kind of person that Jonny was, he was practically in tears recalling their conversation. He indicated that she had tried persuading him to give it another shot, but his mind was made up. I knew Jonny felt particularly guilty about having plans to go to St. Paul for a wedding with another person before he had officially ended things. So guilty, in fact, that I didn't hear a peep from him for the next three weeks.

On week four of no word from Jonny, I called Reff and declared that I wasn't going to Sarason's wedding.

"He's obviously second guessing his decision to ask me and he's probably not over his ex. I'm going to end up regretting this trip. Besides, there is no way I'd be able to use a shared bathroom with him anyway given my newly designed digestive system. Speaking of which, I don't even know the room situation. Are we going to have two double beds? A king?"

The Reff told me to calm down. That like me, Jonny was probably overthinking it all, and he perhaps was feeling guilty about his breakup, not to mention dealing with being single again. His absence and lack of communication most likely had nothing to do with me. He was the one that ultimately decided to invite me as his date, right? This was true. That said, if I was going as someone's date to a wedding that weekend, I kind of wanted that date to be someone I felt comfortable with, not someone who was having second thoughts about asking me to go with them.

It was a disaster.

I would simply call Jonny and give him an out. He didn't have to worry about me. There would be other plans for me that weekend. I'd tell him that I wasn't ready to go to another wedding that weekend after all. No harm, no foul. Take lots of pictures and tell me all about it. No need for all the discomfort.

Only when I called him up to say my very well rehearsed speech, he didn't let me get very far. I was somewhere between, "I'll pay you back for the flight and I'm just going to head up to my sister's for the weekend" when he interrupted.

"I'm such an idiot," he said. "Can you meet for dinner tonight? What are you doing?"

A couple hours later we were sitting at a Hillstone restaurant, artichoke spinach dip before us. Jonny apologized for being radio silent over the last several weeks. As Reff predicted, his mind had been occupied over his breakup. He knew it was the right decision, but he didn't like hurting his ex-girlfriend. Being together for over a year, he was relearning how to be single again. He also made sure to tell me several times that he was very glad I was going to the wedding with him, that we would have a great time and to please forgive him for being MIA.

So I was going to this wedding after all.

CHAPTER 12

When we finally showed up at the St. Paul, Minnesota hotel, we walked into the lobby and immediately came face-to-face with Paul Fishman. Strangely enough, my former boyfriend of five years was front and center at check-in at the very second we walked into the hotel. Paul was attending the wedding not only as a guest of Sarason's, but as the date of one of the bridesmaids. It was always slightly tense to see Paul, despite having broken up with him seven years earlier. More recently, we had bumped into each other at fundraiser events or informal gatherings, always with that edge of intensity still present. There is no simple way to interact with an ex-boyfriend I had devoted five years of my life to and loved deeply for a while. Paul gave me one of his clumsy bear hugs and was virtually silent in front of his date.

Jonny and I checked in and headed upstairs to our hotel room. I was simultaneously relieved and disappointed to see that there were two double beds inside. So this was going to be a platonic weekend after all.

After the rehearsal dinner, we met up with several more camp friends who had arrived later at the hotel lobby bar. Over drinks and beer nuts, we relived the glory days, reminiscing about early, cold morning "polar bear" swims in the lake, day hikes to Mt. Hackensack while eating G.O.R.P. (Granola, Oats, Raisins and Peanuts) and the highlights of tribal war, one of the biggest events in summer camp.

Every Sunday in camp, the entire population was divided into two teams—the green Iroquois versus the gold Mohawks who would battle in a series of events, the most exciting of which was Sachem basketball. At that event, the entire camp gathered around at night to watch the oldest (and most eligible) male campers compete in a full-court basketball game. The referee of the game took pleasure in keeping the score very close until the last five minutes. This made the competition extremely heated. The summer that we were 16, the camp rented out the local high school gymnasium where they bussed the entire population of over 600 campers to watch the game. Every girl had on their cutest green or gold fitted tank top and matching zinc oxide on their faces. Music and posters filled the gymnasium during the pre-game warm-ups. The air was electric. When the game finally began, the screaming and coordinated cheers echoed throughout the bleachers. I can clearly remember Jonny in his forest green mesh tank top making layups. The whole crowd would chant his name anytime he had the ball.

At some point during the game, Jonny got elbowed in the face. Blood squirted from his mouth, all over the floor, and the 6-foot-2 lanky forward went down hard. Time out was called as someone from the health center rushed over, assessing the damage. With the entire camp chanting his name in the background, Jonny was escorted off the court. Turns out he bit through his tongue but no stitches were needed.

Every camp friend sitting in that hotel lobby bar after Sarason's rehearsal dinner had been at that legendary Sachem basketball game. Jonny referred to that night with the roaring crowd screaming his name as the highlight of his teenage life—"blood and all."

The after-party was winding down, and I suddenly started to feel nervous. We had certainly chatted together throughout the night, but I had absolutely no indication from Jonny that our trip to St. Paul was any sort of a romantic venture. Regardless, we were having a great time, and I decided that it had been worth it after all—romance or no romance. How nice to catch up with old friends, including Jonny. How easily I had been distracted. It was always the case that an actual dreaded event was never as bad as anticipated.

The would-be wedding did sit on my shoulder that weekend, whispering into my ear every now and then, "This would have been your rehearsal dinner night…" Of course, if it were my rehearsal dinner night, I would have been one step closer to walking down the aisle toward someone who doubted whether they wanted me to be their life partner.

And somehow, I realized over the course of the evening that it was OK. Strangely, impossibly, I was happy to be where I was for the first time in so long. I had taken it all in—the anticipated, re-lived heartache, the loss, the broken plans. For once it was fine having no idea what was coming next.

It was almost six hours since the rehearsal dinner and we were hungry again. Jonny and I headed up to the hotel room and ordered room service. The hunger and exhaustion from a long day took over the anxiety of whether anything would happen between us. I was simply enjoying a fun night out with old friends, to be topped off with late-night chicken quesadillas, some French fries and a Diet Coke. I traded in my navy blue cotton dress for an old camp T-shirt and mesh shorts, something I easily could have worn to the camp canteen 14 years earlier. As we waited for the food to arrive, we recapped the night, our conversations with various friends and the peculiar interactions with certain guests.

"You know Fishman asked me if we had a king-sized or double beds," Jonny said.

"No he didn't!" I said. "What did you say?"

"I told him we had bunk beds," he said. "Are you sure you guys aren't still dating?"

"They never forget," I joked. "Ah well, he seems happy now with his new girlfriend."

The feast arrived and we quickly chowed down the late night greasy snacks. After the last bite was consumed, I brushed my teeth, washed my face and dove into one of the double beds.

Jonny must have been equally exhausted, because when he emerged from the bathroom minutes later and jumped into the other bed, we were both sleeping within minutes. His sound snoring confirmed what I already suspected: We were officially on a platonic date for the weekend.

CHAPTER 13

My eyes popped open around 8:00 AM. It was August 25th, my canceled wedding day. My first act was to run off to the bathroom and eliminate any evidence that I could possibly have morning breath. I washed my face, brushed my hair and put on a tiny bit of cherry-flavored ChapStick. If actresses could look good upon first waking up in the morning with fully styled hair and flawless makeup, why couldn't I primp a bit?

With the curtains drawn over the floor-to-ceiling windows in our hotel room, it was still pitch-black in the room. I tiptoed with my hands out, blinded by the darkness upon coming out of the bathroom. Quietly shuffling closer to my bed, I wondered how much longer Jonny would sleep. I considered just jumping on top of him while he was sleeping, attacking him with kisses before he could even open his eyes and think too hard about what was happening. But if he wasn't remotely feeling the way I was, this could make for a very awkward rest of the weekend.

I continued the blind pilgrimage from the bathroom directly to my bed on the far side of the room. About three steps in, I got a pillow thrown at my head. This triggered an instant pillow fight. Which then led to some light wrestling. My face instantly felt flushed and my heart was beating out of my chest. I couldn't remember the last time I felt this way—giddy, excited and hopeful. The wrestling led to tickling. Our faces were inches apart. He stopped torturing me for just a second and instead leaned in to kiss me. It was gentle at first, but when it was determined that the kissing was not an accident and that we were not in a Saratoga motel surrounded by eight of our friends, it continued into what I had been waiting for from Jonny for the past 12 years.

And that was the start of how the morning of my almost wedding day turned into my first date with Jonny. To protect the sanctity of that moment, the details must be spared, but suffice it to say, there was no breakup speech a few minutes later.

As a groomsman in the wedding, Jonny had until noon to report to the groom's suite. Which gave us a couple of hours to go to brunch and recover from the line that had just been crossed. We ended up going to the St. Paul Diner around the corner from the hotel and had one of the biggest and cheapest breakfasts known to mankind. There is a picture of me somewhere with very flushed cheeks, messy hair and the biggest grin I'd ever had during that breakfast of champions.

The rest of the wedding weekend was exactly what I needed—the distraction of camp friends, a budding romance with Jonny and enough awkward interactions with Paul Fishman to make me forget that I could have been at my own wedding that weekend. On our flight home, I asked Jonny to join me at the US Open the following week since I had an extra ticket and knew he liked tennis. It felt like I had held my breath for three days until he called to say that he'd love to join. In between sets during an intense match under the lights, Jonny returned to our seats with a US Open journal.

"For all the great writing you're going to do," he said.

Out of all the jewelry, spa treatments and even the platinum diamond engagement ring Brad had bought me, nothing was as "me" as that journal.

During the next several weeks, Jonny and I hung out a handful of times—watching TV at his apartment, catching a movie or going for Mexican food. We never said a word about what was or wasn't going on between us, but I knew that he was struggling with it.

A few weeks after Sarason's wedding, Jonny sent a quick email that I should stop by his apartment after work. He didn't say we should grab dinner or watch a movie or anything to indicate what he had in mind. I was convinced a speech was coming. He was ready to have it out. I knew this would have to take place eventually, but I had hoped for a little more time to see where things would go between us.

As soon as I walked into his apartment, I knew something had changed. Jonny seemed a bit more reserved and made sure to keep at least five feet away from me at all times. One of his roommates was home, so after a few minutes of chatting about the weather, the cab ride over and other meaningless topics, he ushered me into his bedroom and shut the door. He pulled out his desk chair and made me sit in it. Then he sat on his bed facing me. I felt my heart racing. This was it.

Jonny started talking about how great a person he thought I was. How much fun he had at Sarason's wedding. That he has learned more about me in the past couple of weeks than he had known in the last 16 years. So far, this was starting off pretty similarly to the talk he had given me back on our Saratoga day off when we were 18 years old. In fact, his words were so alarmingly similar that they brought an immediate smile to my face. Jonny stopped speaking to ask why I was grinning, at which point I told him to just continue.

"I just got out of a serious relationship. Part of me thinks that I should take some time to be single. To clear my head. I wasn't expecting for things with you to start so suddenly and I know that given where I am right now, I can't just jump into something serious with you. And you can't just casually date Stacey Becker," he said.

Although disappointing, I knew that Jonny was being perfectly honest and showing his respect for me.

"Look," he continued, "You have been through some horrible stuff this past year. The last thing that I want to do is to put you through the same type of situation you went through with Brad. I know that at this point I'm not ready to be in another serious relationship and I am not even sure if…"

"OK, OK," I interrupted. "Now it's my turn to talk. If you're not interested in me…if you only see me as a friend and nothing more…I'm OK with that, but just be honest with me."

"It's not that," he said, "I like you. I have so much fun with you. I'm attracted to you. I just don't want to hurt you any more than you've been hurt. And I'm not sure it would even work out with us…"

Still smiling, I got up from his desk chair, took one of his hands and said, "So, you kind of need a singles vacation to clear your head, right?"

"Something like that," he said.

"You want to go to bars, watch hours of uninterrupted football, eat nachos, wings and drink beer with your buddies and hit on lots of girls?" I asked.

He just looked at me, not sure whether to laugh or remain serious.

"I agree with you," I said. "That's what you should be doing at this point. It's the kind of stuff that I should be doing as well. Wild oats sowing and all that good stuff," I said.

Jonny seemed taken aback by my words and calmness. He clearly did not expect this sort of reaction. Truthfully, I was very OK with what he had just told me, because he was right and I knew that jumping from his recent breakup into a new relationship with a person who was just starting to get her life back on track was probably not the answer.

"So no hard feelings?" he asked, rubbing my hand with one of his fingers.

"None," I said. "Should I help you pack for your singles vacation?" I teased, the concerned look on his face now completely gone.

He laughed, and our heads were inches apart. A large weight had been lifted from both of us. He had ended our budding romance guilt-free and I was no longer expecting a bomb to be dropped on me at a moment's notice—it had already been dropped. For a moment, we were ourselves again, making jokes, laughing and actually flirting. Five minutes after we ended whatever it was that had started in St. Paul, we were kissing.

He pulled away almost instantly, mumbling something about how we probably shouldn't do this anymore and I agreed with him. Then we continued to kiss anyway. A couple of hours later, I wished him well on his vacation, kissed him on the forehead and walked out of his apartment. For me, that was the end of my relationship with Jonny.

It was over.

I would not sit around and wait for him to have an epiphany that would never come. I was done thinking of witty, short emails that would prompt a response from him. Never again would I wait for someone to decide whether they wanted to be with me. They either did or they didn't—the gray area just didn't work anymore. At least this made it easier to figure out my next move. It was time to start getting back out there, to move on. I was done chasing Jonny, or anyone for that matter.

CHAPTER 14

There were a few orders of business that needed to be taken care of now that I was recovered from the surgery, back at work full time and there were absolutely no romantic prospects to date in sight. The first was finding a new place to live. Being in the same apartment where I had lived with Brad was less than ideal for a number of reasons. First off, there was nobody to split the high rent with. Second, the neighborhood was extremely quiet, particularly for New York City, with little but the gym a block away to keep it interesting. Third, I had thrown myself into the online dating world and went out a couple of times with a cute real estate agent—what was the point of doing that if I couldn't employ his services for a bit? Our limited flirtation had transitioned into a fun friendship and we'd still go out for the occasional dinner. The search was on to buy a one-bedroom apartment—something close to a park for jogging purposes, a short distance to the subway for commuting and that would not leave me bankrupt. It was hard to believe that 800 square feet in Manhattan could cost the same as a 3,000-square-foot house in the suburbs.

Finding the perfect apartment in Manhattan was no different than seeking out compatible qualities in a long-term mate. Both searches required being savvy enough to avoid the hidden land mines, keeping faith that eventually the perfect match would come along and having the courage to walk away when the deal went south.

As soon as I walked in the door of the mid-East 70s Street doorman building apartment, I knew that I'd be making a bid. It was perfect. Sunlight poured into the enormous living room, reflecting off the wooden parquet floors. The galley kitchen had a large window, beautiful cherry wood cabinetry, granite countertops and stainless steel appliances. There was a pass-thru window above the oven that overlooked the living room. The bedroom was enormous, easily able to accommodate a king-sized bed and it had multiple windows, one of which overlooked Second Avenue. There was a pocket door leading to a fully renovated marble bathroom in the bedroom while the half bathroom sat off the living room. The best part of the entire apartment was the closet space. The previous owner had installed a walk-in closet as well as two additional California closets. This was the first time in a while that anything from California appealed to me.

My offer was accepted and contract negotiations began. The apartment was a perfect fit. The last step was meeting with and getting approval by the co-op board. After I submitted an obscene amount of paperwork, two male board members interviewed me as we all sat on lounge chairs on the building's rooftop. They told me that the co-op's residents were more of a "dinner party type crowd" rather than "wild keg party types." They questioned which category I fell into.

I debated telling them that I was somewhere in the middle but opted for, "I work at Lehman. Who has time for dinner or keg parties?"

They seemed to like that answer as I received board approval and was cleared to schedule a closing. At the closing, my real estate attorney commented that I would probably have my first baby in that apartment. How far off something like that seemed.

My new apartment was wonderful. My sister took over the choosing of paint colors in the living room and bedroom. I told her that I wanted something cheerful that would put me in a good mood when I entered. Wendy picked a pale yellowish color for the bedroom and some version of pink sand for the living room. She said it would feel like I was at the beach. Besides having to hire a couch doctor to split my couch in half to get it through the doorway of the new apartment, everything else fit pretty well. Including the high-definition flat screen TV that I refused to let Brad take. I also found a place for my rotating rainbow light disco ball in case I decided to throw a wild keg party or maybe as a festive centerpiece for a mature, responsible dinner party.

When the last box was unpacked, I included Jonny on a group email informing friends of my move and updated address. That did get an email back from Jonny congratulating me and asking when he would get to see the new place. A couple of nights later, Jonny was sitting on my couch watching TV after dinner in my new neighborhood. I tried to gauge whether in the past six weeks since I had last seen him he regretted ending what we had started at Sarason's wedding. It was a work night, and despite my best efforts to remain available for flirtatious conversation, I somehow drifted off to sleep while watching TV. I woke up to Jonny getting ready to leave.

"Wait," I said. "I'm just resting my eyes. I'm up now."

"Go to bed," he said. "It's late and you have work tomorrow."

"But," I stammered, trying to think of any reason for him to stay, "I have to show you something in my bedroom," I managed to get out, regretting the words as soon as they escaped my mouth.

He smiled, fidgeted with a button on his coat, and headed toward the door.

"Goodnight, Stace. I love your place. It's like the Ritz-Carlton compared to where I live."

He opened the door, walked out and was gone, back to his singles vacation. Leaving me the entire night to wonder how I had fallen asleep with the object of my affection sitting on the couch next to me. Some hostess I was.

Over the next few weeks, I became more social than I had been in the last few years. A small group of my coworkers invited me to join their indoor soccer team to compete against other Lehman teams once a week in cramped, smelly gyms all over Manhattan. I had absolutely no interest (or talent) in soccer, but it was a great way to meet new people and it made work more of a social outlet. I regularly went to happy hour, to weekend parties, barbecues—any chance to go out and meet new people.

A coworker set me up with a college friend of hers who had recently gotten out of a relationship as well. He was training for the upcoming New York City marathon and I thought that we would at least have that to talk about. But all he wanted to discuss was his financial job at Goldman Sachs and disclosures in the earnings that had been released. Not interested.

I continued with the online dating search, going on a string of first dates that never led to anything more. I met Important Business Guy. He was on his cell phone doing a work call from the moment we met up until our appetizers arrived. He spent ten minutes giving me his resume and another five naming people at Lehman Brothers that he knew. I eventually called a friend from the bathroom who agreed to call a few minutes later to fake an emergency that her cat got electrocuted.

A college friend dragged me to a speed-dating event where I met Aaron. He lived at home with his parents, worked with his dad and spoke only in the third person.

"When Aaron wants something, he goes after it," he said over dinner at Uva, a neighborhood Italian restaurant.

Stacey was not interested.

I did get to date two with Stuart. He was Canadian, tall with a great smile and showed up on our first date wearing a sports jacket, a skinny tie, designer jeans and polished penny loafers. He gelled his dark wavy hair heavily and it looked so crisp and perfectly sculptured that I resisted reaching out across the dimly lit bar to see if my fingers could make a pinecone crunching sound by pinching it.

I watched his mouth as he talked, which I could have sworn had a light lip gloss on them, or else he must have kept wetting his lips because they glistened constantly against the light from the bar's fireplace. Stuart gave me his war stories of online dating. *The women never looked like their pictures. They were only interested in wealthy traders or doctors or lawyers. Their profiles always stated things like, "I'm just as comfortable in a ball gown as in a T-shirt and sweatpants."*

This was never true, he declared emphatically, as who is more comfortable in a ball gown than sweatpants?

He was serious like his name—Stuart—but had a quiet charm about him. There were awkward pauses in between conversation topics as I wondered if I looked like my profile picture and if any of my online profile essays revealed being comfortable in sweatpants. He gave me a shy peck on the lips after our first date.

Our second and last date took place at a comedy club preceded by grabbing slices at a casual local pizza restaurant next door. I had come straight from work and was starving. As soon as Stuart saw me walk into the pizza place, he went straight to the counter to place our order.

Instead of saying hello to me, he greeted the pizza counter guy with a, "I'll take three plain slices and a Coke."

Three slices were put into the oven. I wasn't sure if he wanted to share the soda, so I ordered my own drink and secured napkins, straws and a quiet table in the back. A few minutes later, Stuart sat down facing me with his tray. I was about to reach across the table to grab one of the three plates containing a giant pizza slice when he said, "Are you going to order anything?"

I waited for him to crack a smile. To indicate that he was kidding. Surely, he wasn't going to eat three gigantic slices of pizza on his own. Wouldn't he have asked if I wanted anything when he went to order if he intended to eat this all by himself? A few seconds passed with no indication of humor.

"Um, yeah," I said. "I'll go order now."

Three minutes later, I returned with my own slice. I was shocked to see that not only had two of Stuart's pizza slices disappeared already, but that he had sauce running up and down his wrists and forearms with strings of cheese interlaced between his pinky and ring fingers. He was three bites into his third slice. The grease had already formed a ring around his shiny lips. Chunks of red sauce stuck to his chin as he hungrily and greedily attacked the remaining slice in a matter of seconds. I wasn't entirely comfortable that any chewing was actually done. He seemed to have inhaled the entire piece at once straight into his body, with grease, cheese string bits and globs of sauce powdering his face as the only remnants.

I offered him napkins, but he turned them down. My hunger waned from witnessing such a grotesque consumption of a once favorite food product. I watched in quiet fascination as he went back to the pizza counter and ordered a fourth slice. Had this guy eaten anything in the past week? Stuart wolfed down the fourth slice of pizza and since I could only stomach a few bites of my own, he happily finished mine off as well. He wiped his oiled fingers on his jeans before running them through his hair. No wonder his hair was so crispy! By the time we got into our seats at the Comedy Club, I was planning my escape route. I much preferred sweatpants to going out with him ever again.

I tried to follow up on some of the better dates I had gone on more recently. Over the next couple of months, I kept busy and forged ahead with life. My focus was dedicated solely to work, getting back into shape and learning how to function as a single, independent female again.

CHAPTER 15

Returning home from a trip to Costa Rica where a conversation with a college friend over a two-hour ping pong match on the beach motivated me to check in with Jonny, I bit the bullet and called him on a Tuesday afternoon from work. It had been nearly two months from his "singles vacation" speech. In response to my dinner invite, he asked me to join him at 7:30 PM the next night at a local Southern-themed barbecue sports bar where he was meeting some male buddies at 8 PM for football watching.

"We'll be able to catch up a bit before everyone gets there," he said.

My heart sank a bit. OK, so this wasn't going to be the romantic one-on-one reunion I had been picturing in my head. Was he sticking to the safety in numbers theory and trying to avoid any awkward alone moments with me? He so knew what I was up to!

"Sure," I said, trying not to sound too disappointed. "Sounds like fun."

I arrived at Brother Jimmy's at approximately 7:25. Jonny had texted that he was already in the back, sitting at the long table reserved next to two gigantic TV screens that would show the game. I took about three steps into the restaurant when I heard someone scream my name from behind. It was Sarason. He had gotten out of work late and decided to come straight to the restaurant. I loved Sarason but had never been so disappointed to see him. So much for the soulful, revolutionary conversation I was hoping to have with Jonny.

Jonny gave me a big hug when we made it to the back room, and I sat in a chair directly across from him. It had been months since the last time I saw him and I had forgotten how it felt to be excited about seeing a male interest. Not only could I feel my entire face light up once we started talking, it felt like my entire body was alive again. The others trickled in closer to the game's start time. The shouting at the TVs began along with loud music at commercial time.

As the guys were exchanging their hellos, shaking hands and ordering beers, Jonny ever so slightly leaned across the table so the others couldn't hear and said, "Why don't you come back to my place after this so we can actually hear ourselves talk?"

A flash of heat flooded up into my face and I prayed that I hadn't turned tomato red in excitement. I simply nodded, which was the closest I came at a response. I tried to remove the perma-smile from my face. For the next three hours, I was in a happy trance as the guys watched, debated and screamed at the television. Thankfully Jonny had invited me back to his apartment at the beginning of the night, because I wasn't sure I could have made it through an entire football game without wondering what the hell I was doing there. The only issue was that it was still a work night, so this catching up would need to take place relatively quickly.

When the game ended we walked back to Jonny's apartment. He put on the TV, which we briefly watched. We chatted about a large range of topics while watching TV: Costa Rica, my new apartment, work and how his auditions were going.

The air between us had this stillness and the scented candle Jonny had lit was still going strong. The lights were off already and he handed me a blanket on the couch. My eyes were starting to get heavy, but I fought the instinct to curl up on his couch and take a nap. We were sitting side-by-side on his couch, 11:45 PM on a Thursday night. Something had to happen sooner or later, right?

This very thought was going through my head when Jonny's roommate burst through the door. He had just finished his film writing class and had come up with an incredible script idea that he had to share with someone. So side-by-side, with the candle lit, Jonny and I became his audience. For the next thirty-plus minutes, his roommate described in painstaking detail and tons of hand gestures, the longest plot of all time. To this day, I have no idea what his movie idea was about. By the time he finished his proposal, I could not open one of my eyes and the other one was fluttering. It was almost 1 AM. Jonny asked me if I had work the next day and once I admitted that this was the case, he suggested that I should probably get going. ARGHHHH.

He pulled me up from the couch, turned off the TV and got my coat for me. Then he walked me out of his building and up the block. There was a blatant silence between us. As we passed a bus stop on the way to the corner, Jonny noticed it had an advertisement for a movie.

"We should see that sometime," he said without making eye contact.

He continued walking about three feet ahead of me without waiting for me to respond. This was getting awkward. As soon as we reached the corner, a taxi appeared with its light on, indicating it was free. Within a span of five seconds, Jonny hailed down the cab, opened the door, guided me into it, shut the door and waved goodbye. A quicker exit could not have been achieved with thirty years of practice.

The entire way back to my apartment I thought about what went wrong, whether I had imagined that there was something still brewing between us that night or if it was just in my head. He seemed interested in catching up, but that could have been Jonny being his friendly self. Hadn't he told me repeatedly for the past 10+ years that he only thought of me in a platonic sense? It was time to move on. Again.

The next morning, it was impossible to get out of bed for work. I was severely disappointed from the previous night and went over every detail backward and forward to determine whether I had missed an opportunity. Had I imagined a spark still there between us? Was I willing a chemistry that simply never existed? By the time I finally headed into the bathroom, there was no time for a shower. Only a quick splash of the face, brush of the teeth and throwing on a suit before heading out the door.

I spent half the morning buried returning emails before going out to grab a quick lunch. When I returned to my desk, I saw a missed call from Jonny on my cell phone. That's strange. Did I forget something at his apartment? Normally, I intentionally do that sort of thing, but this time I had been too tired to come up with anything that creative.

But when Jonny answered the phone and asked me how work was going, I knew instantly that this was not at all about something I had left behind.

"I'm going to throw a curve ball at you," he said.

I liked where this was going.

"There's this new movie coming out today and I was thinking maybe we could go see a 4:45 PM IMAX showing of it," he said.

I paused. Completely taken off guard. Did he just ask me to do something with him in the middle of a Friday?

"Ohwowhmmmm," I said, not able to think of any English words to adequately respond to the question he just asked me. Then I remembered that I was wearing a suit, sitting at my desk in an office.

"You know it's a workday, right?"

"Yeah, I know," he said. "I figured maybe you could leave a little early? It's Friday."

I didn't spend a half a second debating what I would do.

"Sure," I said. "I'll need to finish up some stuff here, but that sounds fun."

"Great," he responded, "so why don't you meet me at my apartment whenever you're done and we'll head over to the movie theater together?"

I grabbed my stuff, cabbed it home, showered and made it to his place in record time. Arriving at Jonny's apartment 11 minutes later by taxi, I walked back into the place I had left 14 hours earlier and sat back on the couch.

"Now where were we?" I said.

That got a smile out of Jonny. We watched some TV for a bit, then went to see the new Steve Carell movie, followed by dinner and a couple of drinks at two different bars in his neighborhood. There was something different about that night. The worrying was done. There was a strange calmness. For some reason it felt like there was much less riding on that particular night and the thousand little moments that had gone into it. I felt something had changed in Jonny, that by his actions (I couldn't remember the last time *he* had initiated making a plan with me) I knew he was giving this a shot.

At the end of the night, we spent about two hours making outlandish facial expressions into the camera of his Apple computer, testing every feature and effect on it. It was way after midnight and I waited, in an amused state, to see how Jonny would make something happen. Because at this point, after all of my attempts and re-attempts, it wasn't going to come from me. Somewhere between the roller coaster ride and trip to Paris with the Eiffel Tower effects in the background of our crazy-faced photos, Jonny's singles vacation came to a halt. There was an initial kiss, followed by my internal, "Holy Cow!" moment, followed by hours of kisses. Jonny offered me pajamas by way of his XL T-shirt and the longest sweatpants I had ever seen in my life. Despite not wanting to share a bathroom with Jonny's two other roommates, things were happening here that I didn't want to miss.

The next morning, I woke up in the same position that Jonny and I had woken up together in Saratoga over 12 years earlier. I could barely keep the grin off my face—had I thought this was a remote possibility 24 hours earlier? Such a difference a day could make. Jonny and I went for brunch at the local diner down his street. Not a word was mentioned about what had happened. No speeches about us needing to stay friends. No "I like you, but I'm interested in a 16-year-old back in camp," which I guess would have been creepy given our age. It was just us, a pair of good camp friends, going for brunch on a December Saturday morning on the Upper West Side.

After brunch, I made a point to say a goodbye without mentioning any sort of request for future encounters together. If this thing had a remote chance of working out, it needed to come from him. I was done doing the chasing. There was no confusion on Jonny's part about how I felt about him—I'm pretty sure I had made that clear over the last 12 years. If he wanted to make something happen between us, I wanted—or rather, *needed*—to see him take action.

And take action he did. Jonny started calling regularly for plans. I let him do all the asking—which he did multiple times per week. Sushi, movies, his place, my place—each time was better than the next. Still, not a word was spoken about where this was going, if anywhere.

On a rainy Sunday night in late December, we ate delivery Chinese food on the couch and watched TV. While sipping on wonton soup, Jonny took the remote control and paused the screen. He turned to me with a slight smile on his face.

"I must be an enigma of confusion to you," he said.

"Explain," I said.

"Well, on the one hand, I feel like I should still be single. I just got out of a long relationship several months ago and am told that I should be out chasing girls, getting phone numbers, hooking up, going on dates and being in several relationships at the same time. I also think it's not fair for you to not be dating other people while I am in this mindset. You've been so laid back about us hanging out and I'm just not sure I'm ready to be in another relationship again."

"OK," I responded, my heart dropping upon hearing that he was still in singles vacation mode.

"Well, then on the other hand, there are other times, when I think…my TV would fit perfectly in the shelving right here and we could take your TV and put it in the bedroom."

"What are you talking about?" I said, wondering if he had really just said what I thought he said. "Why would my TV automatically get sent to the bedroom? I happen to have an awesome TV. I fought for that TV!"

We spent the next few minutes jokingly arguing about television location before I had the nerve to address what Jonny's words actually meant.

"Well, it sounds like you have some pretty strong conflicting feelings," I said. "Guess you'll need to figure that out," I responded. "And either way, it will be fine."

It was the first time I honestly meant it. I had been through rejection, walked the fires of not knowing what comes next and had come out the other side alive. It really would be fine.

It seemed as if a weight had been lifted off Jonny's shoulders. Perhaps being able to talk about this state of split emotions was the pathway for figuring out what he wanted.

"Look, bottom line is that I really like you, Stace. And it's freaking me out a bit. But I'm not sure I'm ready for all of this. Just be a little patient with me, OK?"

For all the speeches that I had dreaded receiving from Jonny, nothing could have prepared me for what he had just said. Half of him wanted to be single and the other half wanted to move in? I thought good progress would be if we started seeing each other more than once a week.

Around mid-January, we went to the movies to see the latest Tom Hanks film. We got there too early and had an hour to kill before the movie started. While sitting in our seats in the dark theater, I made the brilliant decision to start the whole "Where is this going?" discussion. It was a total disaster.

"So Jonny," I said, "we've been hanging out now for about six weeks, spending lots of time together and I think we can agree it's been great, right?"

"Uh-huh," he said, checking his iPhone.

"So, well, I don't know. I'm just kind of wondering if you had any thoughts on what's going on between us and where you see it going," I said.

Immediately, he rubbed his face, stammering, "Do you really want to talk about this now? OK, fine. Look, I'm not really sure where things are going. I'm still not sure if I'm ready for a relationship. I'm well, I'm kind of like…until I'm really sure, I don't want to hurt you and commit if I'm not 100% ready. Does that make sense? Hey, are you mad? Don't be mad. Well, wait, I wasn't prepared to start talking about this in a dark movie theater. Can we discuss this later? Don't be upset. We'll talk about it."

His long-winded response made me immediately angry, hurt and wondering why I was wasting any more time with a confused person. Just as I was having this thought, the lights dimmed and the coming attractions started. For the next two-plus hours, we sat in the dark. To this day, I have no idea what that movie was about. My head was stewing.

After the movie, Jonny suggested we go grab some food and talk. We ended up at a burger place near the theater.

Once we had ordered our food, he poured ketchup on his plate for the fries and said, "Look, Stace. You have to know I like and care about you. But I can't tell you at this exact moment that I am entirely ready to be in a relationship, especially not knowing where that relationship would go. I don't think it's fair to you, given everything you've been through. I need more time to think. I'm sorry."

"You know, it's not really that complicated," I said. "All the thinking. The worrying. The back and forth. It shouldn't be that difficult."

The rest of the meal was spent in awkward silence. As soon as the bill came, I paid it, grabbed my coat and walked out of the restaurant. The first available cab got flagged down in an instant and I was home in my pajamas within fifteen minutes. More than anything, I was disappointed. What more did Jonny need to see from me to know if what we had was what he wanted? He knew me well enough to make the decision already. Having the recent experience of dealing with a very confused ex, one thing was crystal clear: I would rather end things completely than spend another second with someone who was confused about how he felt about me.

I went home that night and started typing an email to Jonny. There is some unwritten rule that you should never put anything in writing while you are angry. I was thinking this very thought as the next round of bitterness came pouring through my fingertips onto the screen in front of me. I started out discussing some of the highlights of our past few weeks together—dinners, outings to Central Park, the US Open, holiday parties we had attended together, Sarason's wedding. All of these events had one common theme: When Jonny wasn't thinking too hard about whether he should be in a relationship with me, we were having a pretty incredible time. Eventually, I got to the point:

There will always be other available women out there for you to date. I can guarantee that there will always be someone prettier, smarter, kinder, taller, thinner, better dancers, better cooks, less gassy and far more intellectual. That is the case no matter if you want to be in a relationship with me or anyone else for the rest of your life. Being with me doesn't have to mean that we are getting married tomorrow. It means, let's see where this goes. It means—hey, we have a great time together, we make each other laugh and we are attracted to each other—or that finally, you might actually see me as more than a friend. How about taking it one day at a time? If we reach a point where we're not happy, we agree to address it and go our separate ways. You are worried about putting me through more pain like the kind I just went through. Does that mean that I should never date anyone again? That I should never take the risk of falling on my face again? Because it's not like you meet someone and then boom, seconds later you are happily married. There is usually a learning curve, a chance to get to try each other on for size. This is a very important piece of the puzzle. Like the corner pieces. In any event, before we start thinking of the horrible ways this thing between us is going to end, perhaps we could go for brunch tomorrow, start over and see how the French toast portion of the meal goes. We could take it from there.

Stacey

PS
Stop over-analyzing this letter.

PPS
Your next move is inviting me to brunch tomorrow

I thought about deleting it. Of keeping it as a safe little nugget snapshot of the inside of my brain at this particular point in my life. I really did mean to click the "save as" button but my subconscious took over and shipped that puppy express mail to Jonny's inbox. When I saw the "sent" message pop on the screen, my heart skipped. Well, there goes nothing. To speak in football language, that was the Hail Mary email of my life.

CHAPTER 16

When there was no immediate phone call, no Jonny at my door that night with flowers, I immediately regretted my actions. Did I really need to start lecturing him on giving things with us a shot? Shouldn't Jonny come to that conclusion on his own? What the hell was he so afraid of? Was it really that confusing? I contemplated calling him up and telling him to delete the email (as if he hadn't read it) or claiming that someone hacked my account.

About an hour later, he called. He began by saying, to my surprise, that he liked the email. It had made him think (*but not too much*, he joked) and he decided after a lot of careful consideration that he would in fact enjoy some French toast with me.

Those were the words I had been waiting to hear.

The next couple of weeks were kind of a blur. A whole new relationship between us took off. He was calmer, confident. When we walked down the street together, he would hold my hand. I knew it was getting serious when he started talking in "We's." When his friends called, he'd be chatting away saying things like, "*We* love Thai food," and "*We* love that show."

My mother always told me that there was a match out there for every person. During times of heartbreak, she would say that somewhere in the world, there was a little boy who would one day be ready to find someone like me. From all the books that I had read, movies I had seen and television shows that I had followed, I thought that love would one day arrive on my doorstep, wrapped in a big red bow. The instant spark and attraction would appear as soon as we gazed into each other's eyes. There would actually be thunderbolts appearing between our faces.

I don't remember there being an actual moment when this happened with Jonny. Perhaps it just crept up on me while I was worried about so many other things. I caught glimpses of it when we went on our first trip as a couple and stopped by his Great Aunt Naomi's home in Florida. I watched how he helped her in and out of the car. He held her hand and supported her back while she walked to make sure the 80+-year-old woman was steady on her feet.

I saw it again when he met my Grandma Lillian for the first time. She held his hand and told him how good-looking he was, whispering a bit too loudly to ask me if he was Jewish. Jonny started singing the Hebrew blessing over wine to prove himself, which made her laugh. If there was ever a worry about what my 30-year-old boyfriend and 100+- year-old grandmother would have to talk about, it vanished instantly. They became fast friends.

My initial love for Jonny resurfaced again when for my 31st birthday, he took the words of "Sixteen Going on Seventeen" from my favorite movie, *The Sound of Music*, and changed them to sing about the things we liked to do together. It was a thousand little things like this that made me go from having a crush on Jonny to loving him as a best friend and partner in life.

Jonny, his flat screen TV and *Star Wars* paraphernalia moved in shortly thereafter. You can take the boy out of his old *Star Wars*-decorated apartment, but you can't take the Darth Vader head to rummage. He did let me get rid of two of his three identical *Star Wars* Trivial Pursuit games. Like most things, this was a work in progress.

Being with someone like Jonny, it became clear very quickly that the type of relationship I had with Brad was not sustainable. How things would have eventually crashed and burned had I been able to "fix" the problems between us. Would I be living in California with our baby, divorced and unable to find a job? I hadn't spoken to Brad again since our last phone call, when I was on the way to yet another first date with someone I met online and he called to inform me that he was engaged and marrying Rebecca before the end of the year. It had only been three months since we ended everything. I was shocked and immediately angry at this nonsense. I screamed at him not to ruin his fiancé's life too and hung up. That was the last time we ever spoke by phone.

Steaming mad for 48 hours, I suddenly realized that I didn't really care what Brad did anymore. It was absolutely liberating. I wasn't trapped inside my own head, pining away for someone that didn't love me back. I knew that there was life after love. Independence. I could walk on my own and be happy. There was also love after love gone awry. Lots of great fish in the sea, I guess.

I had assumed that Brad and Rebecca had gotten married as planned. Around the time Jonny moved in with me, Brad, a long lost ghost that no longer haunted me, sent me an email on Facebook requesting to be his friend. As if we were childhood buddies from high school who had a math class together or something. Did he think we could just reconnect? Wish each other "Happy Birthday!" on our Facebook walls and say "Congrats!" when one of us had a baby down the road and posted a photo? I was sure there were more open-minded, altruistic souls out there, but I was not one of them. These experiences gave me an intolerance for superficiality of any kind. Brad sent me a message later the same day indicating that he was now single. The marriage had ended around six months after it began. Brad's words to me in that communication, "Note to self: Don't marry the rebound girl."

I felt a tinge of vindication, then guilt that his divorce gave me any sense of pleasure. The real victim was the poor girl he had married. She had no idea what sort of hurricane she was sucked into. I fought against the urge to reach out to her. Of wanting to console the broken heart that matched my own not so long ago. But I didn't know how to start a conversation with her and sometimes it's best to leave painful memories right where they happened. I had better things to keep me occupied. I should be thanking Brad every day for dumping me. Sure, the roller coaster ride along the way was hell, but it got me to Jonny. There was not enough gratitude in the universe for that turn of events.

If I ever run into Brad in the future, I'd love to give him an unflustered speech evidencing no hard feelings. It would go something like this:

I forgive you, Brad. I thank you for the good times and for helping me discover just how strong I can be. I am especially thankful that you were brave enough to call the whole thing off when it was

*not working and would not work for you. That you didn't waste
my time any longer and enabled me to go off, heal and find a
better fit for myself. I hope you can do the same some day, if you
haven't already. You have allowed me to find the kindest, most
loving and decent love that I ever could have imagined for myself.
Did I mention that he also happens to be gorgeous? By the way,
in case you haven't realized this yet, he often tells me that you
dropped the winning lottery ticket.*

OK, so maybe that last part is just to give a little kick in
the gut, but so be it. I'm only human, and *my* gut has been
through enough.

A year after Jonny moved in, we drove up to visit Echo
Lake and walked past the basketball and hockey courts
into a newly constructed wooden lodge. On the back deck
of the building, Jonny took dozens of pictures of the tall
pine trees, the perfectly round, cotton ball clouds hanging
over the lake used for swim tests. We had both grown up
in that lake – spending so many summers there. He got
into a catcher's position and started taking close-ups of
my face. I raised my hands in protest but Jonny insisted
on seeing me. When I took my hands down, he was
holding out an engagement ring.

My whole body was beaming. Jonny was going to be my
husband and nothing could have made me happier.

We decided to do a destination wedding in San Juan,
Puerto Rico and kept things small and relatively simple.
The majority of the plans were made a month before the
wedding. We never even met the band, florist, wedding
cake baker, hair & makeup person and a bunch of the
other vendors until the day of the wedding. That was
fine with me. It's much less stressful to plan a wedding

knowing that the groom will show up. The weekend was perfect.

We are now married.

When Jonny calls me at work (at my new job since Lehman went bankrupt—a story for another day), he hangs up the phone each time with a "Love you." It's still slightly bewildering. Perhaps I spent so much of my life pursuing guys or hoping to fix a broken relationship that I'm still not familiar with this feeling of contentment. To think that the 18-year-old Jonny who I've had a crush on for all those years is now my husband! Clark Kent is all mine. And now that I'm here, it is clear as day that the past relationships were unacceptable. Relationships may require a bit of maintenance here and there, but if they're problematic before marriage, it doesn't bode well for their future.

As for my own health, so far so good. I have regular check-ups, scans and blood tests to monitor myself. My father and Jonny have stopped coming to every single appointment and reporting full updates to my mother and sister—a sure sign I must be healthy enough for now.

Jonny and I spent the first three years of our marriage traveling, working and catching up on lost time. We then brought home a puppy, Wally, a male Cavalier King Charles Spaniel. We had no idea how to raise a puppy, but there's no denying how fast this little guy became a part of our family. During the summer, Jonny and I regularly go running on the bridle path in Central Park. We bring Wally there on the weekends and let him chase squirrels or birds to his heart's content. Jonny usually wears a *Star Wars* T-shirt and occasionally the three of us relax on the southern end of the Great Lawn where they allow dogs. While Wally licks our faces, Jonny and I lie side by side, staring at the clouds and inventing alternate excuses for the pink, puffy, vertically lined scar on my midsection. Our favorites: shark bite, gang ritual and ill-fated swordfight. He often traces his fingers up and down my Frankenstein-like closed wound, remarking how fortunate he feels that I'm alive.

Time moves fast when you're with the right person. Jonny and I returned to Mt. Sinai Hospital recently for a much happier occasion: the birth of our baby daughter, Ellie Lila. She was a peanut at five pounds, eight ounces, but she's got powerful lungs and the ability, like her father, to completely overwhelm every cell in my body with love and grace. Her dark hair and light eyes immediately reminded me of her father. A mini-Jonny to love. A loving human sister to Wally. What they don't tell you in all those baby books is that the second that little life enters the world, parents are born too.

Everything that came before that moment seems a bit cloudy.

If you leave Ellie alone with any stuffed animal, book or another baby boy, she will attack it with kisses. Jonny says she gets her boy-chasing aggression from her mother. I say that she's just overflowing with the love we've put into her and has no choice but to kiss everything in sight. Each night, I rock baby Ellie to sleep in her nursery and sing her the Echo Lake alma mater. Within a few months of repeating this ritual, her eyes start to close as soon as I'm done with the first few lines. Jonny sits across the room from me, chiming in with Wally on his lap.

He will follow up my singing with the humming of an instrumental version of a *Star Wars* song. Watching Jonny become a father has launched my crush on him to epic proportions. We are completely exhausted at all times and have forgotten what sleeping in feels like, but I have never felt more alive or been more in love with my family than I am these days.

It was worth getting dumped *and* the twelve-year wait for that second kiss.

ACKNOWLEDGEMENTS

This one's for you, Ma. You once told me that somewhere out in the world there was a special someone waiting to meet me. You taught me that when this special someone takes a little longer to show up than we'd like, life goes on in marvelous other ways and it's up to us to go out and soak it all up. Thank you for being my loving mother, incredibly devoted working mom role model and friend. Now that I see what goes into keeping a toddler alive, I could not be more appreciative of the million little things you've done for our family. I love you.

Additional "thanks" go to the following super humans:

My big sister Wendy, who literally breathed for me during this break-up and helped put me back together when I didn't think it was possible.

My charming, young-looking father, Da, your unconditional love never ceases to amaze us. Our bad times have always been your bad times, so let this book be your celebration.

My brother-in-law, David Feldman, and four nephews – Jonah, Ryan, Michael & Andrew – who never let a dull moment exist (an instant elixir for heartache, btw).

Uncle Norman, Aunt Arlene, Diane Edelstein and the rest of my extended family.

My volunteer editors – Amie Long, Erika Vogel and Lauren Adler

My "friend army" that got me through that year: Winetz, Reff, Edelstein, Kruse, Neha, Kimi, Berger, Nyieri, Alana, Mika, Jill, Saroff, Jen the Intern, Amena, MacGregor, Kim, Lauren, Shelley, Leiv, Shari and Robb Malin.

My agent, Emmanuelle Morgen, for the opportunity to get this story out there.

My Thought Catalog book editor, Mink Choi, for taking the "lawyer" out of my writing and forcing me to give it more "Stacey." Thank you for taking a chance on me!

Jonathan. You're "booked" to be the hero in this one. You've been the best journey's end since I returned from the Dark side. Your endless devotion to the Washington Redskins and Capitals has given me hours of writing time.

Ellie Lila. You are my everything. Read this after your first big heartbreak and know that you are strong enough to have everything you want.

ABOUT THE AUTHOR

Stacey Becker is a 30-something writer who lives with her very tall, Star Wars-loving husband in New York City along with their baby daughter and equally cute dog, Wally. Disguised as a corporate lawyer, Stacey circumvents any serious legal discussions in favor of analyzing relationships, her relatable day-to-day adventures and trashy television. She blogs about these topics at http://OfficeStace.com.